Published by Miraivant Press
Rockville, Maryland, United States
Paperback ISBN: 979-8-234-06763-0
Hardcover ISBN: 979-8-9958881-9-2
eBook ASIN: B0GY6TBMJ9
First edition, 2026

This book reflects the perspectives and experiences of the author. It is intended for informational and educational purposes and does not constitute professional, legal, or financial advice.

For speaking engagements and inquiries:
www.miraivant.com

Printed in the United States of America

THE POWER — of — 20%

Stop Surviving Your Week. Start Thriving in It.

How to Identify, Protect, and Amplify
the Work That Makes *You Extraordinary*

BY

ANDREW RAM
BITTAN

Contents

Dedication

Every person I have ever crossed paths with has left something behind. The ones who lifted me, the ones who challenged me, the ones who made the road harder — all of them shaped these pages. The good gave me belief. The bad gave me clarity. The difficult gave me opportunity. They are the frame, the fuel, and the fire.

To my parents — who left Trinidad for a country that didn't know them yet, certain their children would have more. My father's relentless perfectionism in his craft sparked something in me I didn't understand until decades later. My mother's voice — always pushing us to be our best — has never stopped. I still hear it. You are the reason any of this was possible.

To my wife — who walked into the Confucius Institute and asked the director a perfectly reasonable question: who is that guy? That question became a conversation, and that conversation became happily ever after. Between our shared roots in Chinese history and culture, we found each other.

To my son — I have watched you grow into the man you are today, and it has been one of the great privileges of my life. I gave you a love of video games. You turned it into a career I only dreamed of.

Preface

Before you begin, I want you to know something: I wrote this book the same way I am asking you to work.

The research, the drafts, the editorial passes, the bibliography, the prompt library: all produced in partnership with AI. Thirty years of hard-won thinking and stories only I could tell — that was my twenty percent. Structure, research, and refinement, handled by AI — that was the eighty. One hundred percent of the outcome would not exist without both.

Before diving in, I would like you to remember one thing: AI can produce extraordinary outputs. What it cannot supply is the human knowledge behind them. Search the internet for mistranslated signs and you will find proof of that within seconds. Here is one, from a park in China:

1. **What the sign says (the mistranslation):**

   > 小草休扈，请勿扖撟
   >
   > *Xiào cào xiū hù, qǐng wù káng jiào*
   >
   > **"Do Not Disturb — Tiny Grass Is Dreaming"**

2. **What it was meant to say (correct Chinese, transliterated):**

   > 小草休息，请勿打扰
   >
   > *Xiào cǎo xiū xi, qǐng wù dà rǎo*
   >
   > **"Tiny grass is resting — please do not disturb"**

3. **What it actually means (the real message):**

   > **"Keep off the grass"**

The result we see is a translation app doing exactly its job — producing what it calculated to be the correct meaning. However, the issue came from the human driving it.

That is what happens when intelligent technology is deployed without intelligent human knowledge behind it. It is happening everywhere right now — in organizations that believe they are using AI but are really just producing sophisticated versions of a dreaming grass sign.

This book is not another treatise on time management. It is an argument for a fundamentally different reorientation: rather than focusing on reducing what drains you, focus with equal ferocity on amplifying what makes you extraordinary. The 80/20 principle has always told us to cut the eighty. What it rarely asks is what to do with the twenty once you have protected it. That is what this book is for.

How to Use This Book

This book moves in five parts: foundation, framework, AI, life, and a thirty-day sprint. At the end of each chapter you'll find a Practical Exercise, an AI Prompt, and Endnotes. The ideas draw from organizational psychology, cognitive science, and management theory. Their purpose is entirely practical: to help you spend more of your professional life doing what only you can do.

Each chapter ends with a practical AI prompt you can use immediately. If you are new to AI tools, no technical experience is required. The most widely used options are ChatGPT, Claude, and Gemini — all work directly in your browser with no installation needed. To use any prompt in this book: open one of these tools, copy the prompt, fill in the bracketed sections with your own information, and send. The surrounding chapter explains exactly what each prompt is designed to do.

The table below shows every tool and framework you will encounter, where it lives, and what it does in plain English. Return to it whenever you need to orient yourself.

Your Framework Map

Step & Location	Tools You Will Use	What Happens
#1 **Discover** Part 1 · Chs 1–3	Energy Ratio Calendar Autopsy	Find out how much genius time you are actually getting. Most professionals discover the answer is 5–15% of their week.
#2 **Map** Part 2 · Ch 4	Zone of Genius 20% Fingerprint Task Taxonomy 20% Map	Name your best work precisely and categorize everything else so you know exactly what to protect and what to offload.
#3 **Protect & Offload** Part 2 · Chs 5–6	Fortress Calendar Delegation Ladder Handoff Protocol	Build structures to defend your genius hours and transfer everything else clearly to others or to AI.
#4 **Amplify & Scale** Part 2 · Chs 7–8	20% Framework Team Genius Map	Go deeper into your best work, use AI to multiply it, and spread your genius farther than your individual output allows.
#5 **Your 30-Day Sprint** Part 5	All of the above, applied week by week	Not more theory — a calendar. Four weeks of deliberate action that will move you from understanding your 20% to living it.

PART I

The 80/20 Truth Nobody Tells You

Most books about the 80/20 principle begin with the same exhortation: cut the eighty. Eliminate the low-value work. Prune the inefficient activities. What those books rarely examine with sufficient rigor is the positive obligation that follows from that pruning: the duty to understand, protect, and expand the twenty. The three chapters in this section build the diagnostic foundation upon which everything else in this book depends.

CHAPTER

1

The Exhaustion Equation

PART I

> *"Energy, not time, is the fundamental currency of high performance."*
> — Jim Loehr & Tony Schwartz, The Power of Full Engagement (2003), p. 5

The Paradox of the Overachieving Underperformer

Across every engagement I have worked, one pattern has repeated itself more than any other. I now call the framework it produced the BPIA Framework — using Business Intelligence and Process Intelligence to define where the AI layer belongs, and where it does not. One such engagement illustrates the whole argument. I joined a company known for its technology platform and discovered that its own team wasn't using it. Escalations — the critical, time-sensitive issues that most directly affect customers and partners — were being tracked in a spreadsheet. This was not an emergency workaround. It was the system.

The problems were immediate and compounding. The file corrupted regularly. Entries sat for weeks without updates or closure. There was no accountability framework, no SLA tracking, no way to see at a glance what was open, what was overdue, or who owned what. And critically, management had quietly ensured the data was not easily accessible to executive leadership. What lived in that spreadsheet stayed in that spreadsheet.

My own manager was frustrated. Not just with the outcomes, though those were bad enough. With the fundamental dysfunction of the process itself: the reporting burden, the manual data management, the complete absence of accountability. The organization was generating noise and calling it management.

I built a new platform. Every escalation record was migrated. SLAs were established for each issue type, creating for the first time a standard against which accountability could actually be measured. Automated reports went out weekly to every stakeholder without anyone having to compile or send them manually. Dashboards were built for both management and executive views real time, glanceable, honest.

The transformation was a direct demonstration of what I would later formalize as the BPIA Framework™. The existing escalation data was the Business Intelligence: it already knew what was broken, but no one could see it clearly. The new platform was the Process Intelligence: redesigning the workflow so information flowed to the right people at the right time. And the automated reporting and dashboards were the AI layer — the tool that made releasing the eighty percent possible, freeing the team to spend their time actually resolving escalations rather than managing a spreadsheet about them.

That is the whole argument of this book, compressed into a single platform migration. I have watched the same shift happen in healthcare systems, government agencies, technology firms, and classrooms. The details are always different. The pattern is always the same. When you clear the eighty percent, the twenty percent does not just survive. Your capability accelerates. And I suspect you already know exactly which eighty percent is yours to clear.

The Neuroscience of Flow and Friction

Few researchers have shaped our understanding of human potential more profoundly than Mihaly Csikszentmihalyi, the Hungarian-American psychologist whose five-decade study of peak experience produced one of psychology's most enduring concepts: "flow" — the experience of complete absorption in work that is hard enough to stretch you, but not so hard it breaks you. His research produced a consistent finding: we feel most alive, most creative, and most productive when our highest capabilities meet a genuine challenge.

> *"The best moments in our lives are not the passive, receptive, relaxing times, although such experiences can also be enjoyable, if we have worked hard to attain them. The best moments usually occur when a person's body or mind is stretched to its limits in a voluntary effort to accomplish something difficult and worthwhile."*
> — Mihaly Csikszentmihalyi, Flow: The Psychology of Optimal Experience (1990), p. 3

Studies of artists, surgeons, scientists, athletes, and professionals across every knowledge-work domain find the same thing: work produced in flow is more creative, contains fewer errors, and is of higher intrinsic quality than work produced in distracted states.

The neurological mechanism is increasingly understood. Flow states are associated with a phenomenon neuroscientists call transient hypofrontality a temporary downregulation of the prefrontal cortex, the brain region responsible for self-monitoring, linear reasoning, and the imposition of habitual cognitive patterns. When the prefrontal cortex quiets, the brain's default mode network, associated with associative thinking, pattern recognition, and creative insight, becomes more active. The brain, in short, becomes a different kind of machine: less careful, more generative; less cautious, more inspired.

By contrast, the cognitive residue left by tasks that don't engage these systems is both real and costly.

Gloria Mark of UC Irvine — whose research on digital distraction is among the most rigorous in the field — found that it takes an average of twenty-three minutes to fully recover attentional focus after a single interruption.

The Hidden Costs of 80% Work

Let's be specific about the costs that accrue when a professional spends most their working hours outside their zone of highest competence and engagement. These costs are typically invisible in conventional productivity measures but are deeply real in their consequences.

Each hour spent on work that doesn't require full engagement teaches the brain to expect distraction — and eventually to seek it. Technology writer Linda Stone called this "continuous partial attention." The worker is present for the task but always seeking distraction.

This mode of working, practiced daily, becomes habitual. Over time, the ability to sustain deep focus on difficult problems atrophies.

The second cost is motivational. Self-determination theory — developed by Edward Deci and Richard Ryan across four decades of research — identifies three psychological needs at the root of what makes work feel meaningful from the inside: autonomy, competence, and relatedness.

Work in the eighty percent typically undermines all three simultaneously.

The third cost is strategic. Every hour a talented professional spends on work below their capability level is an hour not spent advancing the strategic agenda of the organization. The misallocation of human talent is not merely a problem for you. It is a structural inefficiency that pervades and impedes the organizations that allow it to persist.

Effort Is Not Output

One of the most persistent and damaging myths in professional culture is the equation of effort with output. This myth, which might be called "the myth of the virtuous busyness," holds that working harder, longer, and with greater visible commitment is the surest path to professional success and organizational contribution. It is, to a significant extent, false.

The value of knowledge work lies not in hours expended but in the quality of thinking applied.

And the quality of thinking available for any task depends, in large part, on whether the thinker is operating within their highest capability and engagement.

> *"There is nothing so useless as doing efficiently that which should not be done at all."*
> — Peter F. Drucker, The Effective Executive (1966), p. 43

Anders Ericsson's *Peak* draws an important distinction between naive practice — simply repeating what one already does — and deliberate practice: targeting the specific capabilities in which one is not yet expert.

Most busy professionals do the former and wonder why they stop improving.

The Practical Exercise: The Energy Audit

Before proceeding to the next chapter, the reader is invited to undertake a five-day Energy Audit. The method is straightforward and the insights it generates are often profound.

For five consecutive working days, maintain a simple log of every task you engage in for more than fifteen minutes. For each task, immediately upon completion, assign one of three ratings: Green (you felt energized, engaged, and in your element during this task), Yellow (the task was neutral, neither energizing nor draining), or Red (the task drained your energy, felt beneath your capabilities, or left you feeling depleted).

At the end of five days, calculate the percentage of your working time occupied by each category. Most professionals, upon completing this exercise for the first time, discover that their Green time constitutes between eight and fifteen percent of their working week. This number, whatever it is, is your baseline. It is the number this book is dedicated to increasing.

The Energy Audit in this chapter has one job: to make the invisible visible. Once you can see your ratio, you cannot unsee it. That moment of recognition is where Chapter Two begins.

AI PROMPT, Chapter 1

Use this prompt to find out which tasks on your list belong to your twenty percent — and which ones are ready to be delegated or automated.

> *"Review my task list for today: [paste your list]. For each item, assess whether this type of task is typically energy-generating, energy-neutral, or energy-draining for a professional whose primary strengths are [describe 2–3 of your core strengths]. For any energy-draining task, suggest whether it could be (a) delegated to a colleague, (b) handled by an AI assistant, (c) eliminated entirely, or (d) batched with similar tasks to reduce context-switching cost. Be specific and honest."*

Endnotes: Loehr, J. & Schwartz, T. (2003). The Power of Full Engagement. New York: Free Press. Csikszentmihalyi, M. (1990). Flow: The Psychology of Optimal Experience. New York: Harper & Row. Mark, G., Gonzalez, V. & Harris, J. (2005). No Task Left Behind? Examining the Nature of Fragmented Work. CHI 2005. Stone, L. (2008). Continuous Partial Attention. lindastone.net. Deci, E. & Ryan, R. (2000). The 'What' and 'Why' of Goal Pursuits. Psychological Inquiry, 11(4). Drucker, P. (1966). The Effective Executive. New York: Harper & Row. Ericsson, A. & Pool, R. (2016). Peak: Secrets from the New Science of Expertise. Eamon Dolan/Houghton Mifflin.

CHAPTER

2

What Is Your 20%?

PART I

> *"Each person has an area of strength... The question is not 'what do you do well?' but 'what do you do unlike anyone else?'"*
> — Marcus Buckingham & Donald O. Clifton, Now, Discover Your Strengths (2001), p. 14

The Geometry of Human Potential

In the year 2009, the therapist and executive coach Gay Hendricks published a slim but incisive volume titled *The Big Leap*: Conquer Your Hidden Fear and Take Life to the Next Level. Drawing on thirty years of clinical and coaching work, Hendricks proposed a conceptual map of human performance that has, in the years since, proven remarkably useful to practitioners across fields. He identified four zones of functioning, which he named the Zone of Incompetence, the Zone of Competence, the Zone of Excellence, and the Zone of Genius.

The Zone of Incompetence holds tasks you perform poorly — no aptitude, no developed skill. The Zone of Competence holds tasks you do adequately, but so could anyone else. The Zone of Excellence holds tasks you do very well, often better than most around you, but without the signature energy of your deepest work.

The Zone of Genius is different in kind. It's where your unique combination of talent, skill, and deep interest produces work that nothing else you do can match.

> *"Your Zone of Genius is the set of activities you are uniquely suited to do. They draw on your special gifts and strengths. In your Zone of Genius, time often seems to*

> *stop. You lose track of it entirely."*
>
> — Gay Hendricks, The Big Leap (2009), p. 46

Hendricks's most important observation is this: most talented professionals live not in their Zone of Genius but in their Zone of Excellence. They are highly rewarded for work that is very good — but not their best.

They are trapped by their own competence. The accumulated rewards, expectations, and identity investments that excellence generates make it psychologically difficult to leave work that is good in pursuit of work that is extraordinary.

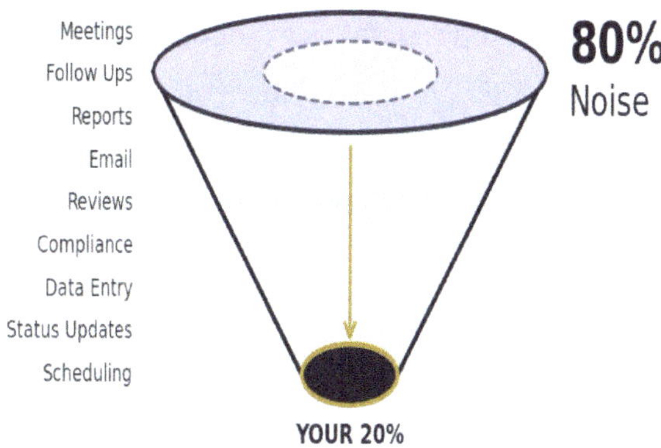

Figure 1 — Your 20%: the zone that must be identified, protected, and amplified

The 20% Fingerprint

What does your twenty percent actually look like? The answer, it must be emphasized, is unique to each person. This is not a rhetorical claim; it is a substantive one. The research tradition associated with positive psychology, and in particular the work of Buckingham and Clifton at Gallup, has generated extensive evidence that human strengths are not distributed on a normal curve but are, instead, highly individuated. Two professionals in the same role, at the same level, in the same organization, may have radically different strengths profiles, and radically different zones of genius.

What these moments share is a consistent signature: time distortion (hours feel like minutes), effortless effort (hard work doesn't feel like a burden), outputs that surprise even the person producing them, and a lingering satisfaction after the work is complete.

That signature is distinct from the satisfaction of merely having finished something.

To identify your twenty percent with precision, the following diagnostic questions are offered not as a definitive instrument but as a starting framework. They are derived from the intersection of Csikszentmihalyi's flow research, Buckingham and Clifton's strengths theory, and the clinical observation of thousands of professionals in coaching and consulting engagements:

First: When, in your working life, have you lost track of time because you were so absorbed in what you were doing? What were you doing in those moments?

Second: What types of problems do your colleagues and clients bring to you, specifically to you, rather than to your peers, because they believe you will handle them better? What does this pattern tell you about your perceived distinctiveness?

Third: What work, when you have completed it, leaves you feeling replenished rather than depleted, even if the work was difficult?

Fourth: What do you understand intuitively, in your domain, that others seem to have to work very hard to grasp?

Fifth: If you could redesign your role from scratch, retaining only the twenty percent of activities you find most alive and meaningful, what would remain?

The Trap of Excellence

For many high-performing professionals, the suggestion that they live primarily in their Zone of Excellence rather than their Zone of Genius provokes a mixture of resistance and grief.

Resistance, because the Zone of Excellence is the source of their external success and professional identity. Grief, because acknowledging it requires confronting how much professional life has been spent at a level below their deepest capacity.

Organizational psychologist Adam Grant, in *Give and Take* (2013), documents a related phenomenon he calls "giver burnout" — the exhaustion that afflicts individuals who give their time and energy without adequate attention to where they create the most distinctive impact.

> *"Being otherish means being willing to give more than you receive, but still keeping your own interests in sight. It means giving in ways that reflect your values and strengths and protect against burnout."*
> — Adam Grant, Give and Take (2013), p. 158

Discovering Your 20% Fingerprint: The Full Exercise

The complete 20% Fingerprint Exercise proceeds in four stages. The first stage is retrospective analysis: identify the five moments in your career that you would describe as your finest professional hours. Not your most recognized, your finest. What were you doing in those moments? What capabilities were you drawing upon? What made those moments feel different from ordinary good work?

The second stage is feedback triangulation: ask three colleagues, ideally people who have worked with you in different contexts, to identify the moments they have observed you operating at a level that surprised or impressed them. Look for patterns across their responses. The external perspective is essential here, because our own twenty percent is often so natural to us that we mistake it for ordinary competence.

The third stage is the effort-to-output mapping. For a period of two weeks, track both the effort you invest in various types of work and the quality of the outputs you produce. You will typically find a striking inversion: the work that produces your best results is often not the work that requires your greatest effort. This inversion is the signature of your Zone of Genius.

The fourth stage is the construction of your Twenty Percent Profile, a single-page document that captures, in your own words, the specific activities, contexts, and problems that constitute your highest contribution. This document becomes the reference point for every chapter that follows.

You now have a name for the work that is uniquely yours. That name is your compass for everything that follows. Chapter Three shows you what has been crowding it out.

AI PROMPT, Chapter 2

Use this prompt to identify the common thread across your proudest professional moments and name your Zone of Genius with precision.

> *"I am going to describe three recent professional moments I'm proud of: [describe them in detail]. After I do, I want you to: (1) Identify the common themes, capabilities, and types of problems that appear across all three; (2) Articulate what appears to be my Zone of Genius based on these examples; (3) Ask me five follow-up questions that will help me sharpen and validate this picture. Begin by analyzing my three examples."*

Endnotes: Hendricks, G. (2009). The Big Leap: Conquer Your Hidden Fear and Take Life to the Next Level. New York: HarperOne. Buckingham, M. & Clifton, D. (2001). Now, Discover Your Strengths. New York: Free Press. Csikszentmihalyi, M. (1990). Flow: The Psychology of Optimal Experience. New York: Harper & Row. Grant, A. (2013). Give and Take: A Revolutionary Approach to Success. New York: Viking.

CHAPTER

3

The Tyranny of the 80%

PART I

> *"The key is not to prioritize what's on your schedule, but to schedule your priorities."*
> — Stephen R. Covey, First Things First (1994), p. 161

The Colonization of Your Calendar

I want to tell you about a project I watched unravel, not because the team lacked talent or the work was too hard, but because of how a single leadership decision turned a calendar into a weapon.

A new manager was brought in mid-project. He had limited experience in the specific field, which is not itself a problem. Leaders often come in from outside. The problem was what he did with his uncertainty. Rather than investing time in understanding how the work actually functioned, he defaulted to the one tool that made him feel in control: meetings.

Multiple times a week. Each one framed as a check-in, a status update, an alignment session. Each one, in practice, a scrutiny exercise. The team, people who had real work to do and a real deadline approaching, found themselves constantly pulled out of deep concentration to justify what they had or hadn't finished since the last meeting.

The outcomes were predictable. Work suffered. Resentment built. Then came the moment that crystallized everything for me. One team member, a seasoned professional who had personally led a previous, similar project, was presenting findings from that earlier engagement. Findings that contained real lessons, hard-won insights that were directly relevant to what the team was trying to build now.

The manager interrupted him midway through. In front of the group, he reframed the previous project as a failure. He listed what had gone wrong. He used it as a cautionary example of what this team needed to avoid.

Here's what was true: the previous project had not failed. It had surfaced exactly the kind of insight that prevents failure downstream. That's not failure. That's the most valuable kind of work a team can do.

What that manager destroyed in that room wasn't just morale. It was institutional knowledge. He used meeting time to invalidate the very experience the team needed to draw on. And the project, predictably, struggled.

I've seen versions of this dynamic in technology companies, healthcare organizations, and government agencies. The details change. The pattern doesn't. When leaders fill the calendar with control rather than clearing it for contribution, the cost is never just time. It's the work that never gets done because the people who could do it were too busy being watched.

Having established what your twenty percent is, we must now reckon honestly with the forces that systematically prevent you from spending time within it. These forces are not random. They are structural, cultural, and in many cases, deeply internalized, which is precisely what makes them so difficult to resist.

The first force is meeting culture. Meetings have metastasized from a useful coordination mechanism into a primary mode of professional existence.

Meeting researcher Steven Rogelberg of the University of North Carolina found that the average knowledge worker spends between thirty and fifty percent of their working week in meetings — with senior leaders reporting even higher proportions.

Cal Newport's *Deep Work* (2016) is blunt about this. Contemporary organizations have rebuilt themselves around open offices, instant messaging, and perpetual availability expectations — and each of those choices actively undermines the deep, focused concentration that high-value knowledge work requires.

> *"Deep work is the ability to focus without distraction on a cognitively demanding task. It's a skill that allows you to quickly master complicated information and produce better results in less time."*
>
> — Cal Newport, Deep Work (2016), p. 3

The 'Always Available' Trap

The expectation of perpetual availability, which has intensified dramatically with the proliferation of email, Slack, and mobile communication, represents a particularly damaging threat to twenty-percent work. This expectation operates, in many organizations, as an invisible but pervasive norm: the professional who does not respond to messages within minutes is perceived as less dedicated, less engaged, or less reliable than one who is constantly connected.

This norm is not merely inconvenient; it is neurologically destructive. Information systems researcher Thomas Jackson and colleagues at Loughborough University found that, following an email interruption, workers' heart rates elevated, their stress indicators increased, and their cognitive performance on complex tasks degraded measurably. The worker who checks email every few minutes does not simply lose the minutes consumed by each check; they lose the quality of attention available for the work that actually requires their best thinking.

Daniel Levitin, in *The Organized Mind*: Thinking Straight in the Age of Information Overload, explains this phenomenon through the lens of attentional resources. The human prefrontal cortex, the neural substrate of our highest cognitive functions, operates on a limited budget of energy and focus. Each switch of attention, each interruption processed, each notification responded to draws on this budget. The professional who allows her attention to be perpetually interrupted is spending her twenty-percent capital on eighty-percent transactions.

The Guilt of Saying No

One of the most psychologically complex dimensions of protecting your twenty percent is the guilt that accompanies the act of saying no to requests, meetings, and demands that are, individually, entirely reasonable. The colleague who asks for your help with their presentation is not asking anything unreasonable. The manager who invites you to a cross-functional planning session is not acting in bad faith. The client who requests a detailed briefing document is exercising entirely legitimate authority.

The problem is not any individual request but the aggregate of all of them, and the way in which that aggregate reliably displaces the work for which you are most uniquely valuable. As Gary Keller and Jay Papasan argue in The One Thing: The Surprisingly Simple Truth Behind Extraordinary Results, the act of saying yes to one thing is always, simultaneously, an act of saying no to something else — and in the context of your twenty percent, that something else is almost always the work that matters most. The question is not whether you will say no, but whether you will say no to the right things.

> *"Saying yes to everyone is saying no to yourself. Every yes you give is a commitment of time you have to deliver on. Say yes cautiously and mean it."*
> — Gary Keller & Jay Papasan, The One Thing (2012), p. 173

Conscientious, high-performing individuals tend to feel personally responsible for the success of any request directed at them, regardless of whether their unique contribution is actually required. Breaking this pattern requires not merely permission to say no but a principled framework that makes the act of saying no feel professionally appropriate rather than personally selfish.

The Calendar Autopsy: A Diagnostic Tool

The Calendar Autopsy is, for most people, the most disturbing exercise in this book. It answers one honest question: of the hours you work each week, what percentage genuinely requires your unique capabilities — and what percentage is everything else?

Most people, when they run this exercise rigorously, discover their actual Twenty Percent Ratio is somewhere between eight and fifteen percent.

Calculate the percentage of total working time occupied by each category. The typical professional, upon completing this exercise, discovers that twenty-percent work, genuine Zone of Genius activity, constitutes between eight and fifteen percent of their working month.

Necessary support work typically accounts for another twenty to thirty percent. The remaining fifty to seventy percent of their professional life is occupied by work that is either delegable or automatable.

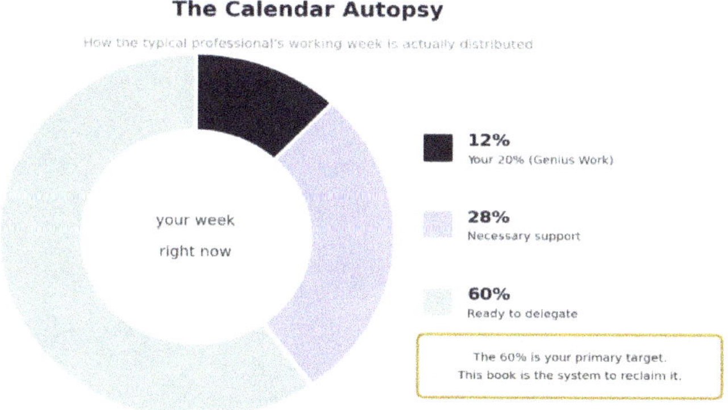

Figure 5 — The Calendar Autopsy: how the typical professional's week is actually distributed

This last figure, the fifty to seventy percent, represents the primary target of the Amplification Framework we will develop in Part Two. It is not merely wasted time; it is time that is actively displacing the work that would create outsized value for the organization and disproportionate fulfillment for the individual.

The Calendar Autopsy does not lie. Whatever your ratio revealed, that number is not a verdict. It is a baseline. Part Two is the system for changing it.

AI PROMPT, Chapter 3

Use this prompt to run a Calendar Autopsy on your recent schedule and find the top changes that would immediately free up genius time.

> *"Here is my calendar from the past two weeks: [paste your schedule in text form or describe the recurring categories of meetings and tasks]. Please analyze it by categorizing each recurring type of activity as: (A) 20% Genius Work, requires my unique capabilities; (B) Necessary Support, must be done but doesn't require my unique genius; (C) Delegable, required my title/authority but not my unique skills; (D) Automatable, could be handled by a process or AI tool. Calculate the approximate percentage of time in each category. Then identify the top three highest-value changes I could make to recover time for Category A work."*

Endnotes: Newport, C. (2016). Deep Work: Rules for Focused Success in a Distracted World. New York: Grand Central Publishing. Rogelberg, S. (2019). The Surprising Science of Meetings. New York: Oxford University Press. Jackson, T., Dawson, R. & Wilson, D. (2003). Reducing the Effect of Email Interruptions on Employees. International Journal of Information Management, 23(1). Levitin, D. (2014). The Organized Mind. New York: Dutton. Keller, G. & Papasan, J. (2012). The One Thing. Austin: Bard Press.

PART II

The Amplification Framework

Having diagnosed the problem in Part One, we are now ready to prescribe the solution. The Amplification Framework is a five-stage system, Map, Protect, Offload, Amplify, Scale, that provides a structured pathway from the diagnostic clarity achieved in Part One to the systematic expansion of your twenty percent. Each stage builds upon the last, and each requires both conceptual understanding and deliberate practical action.

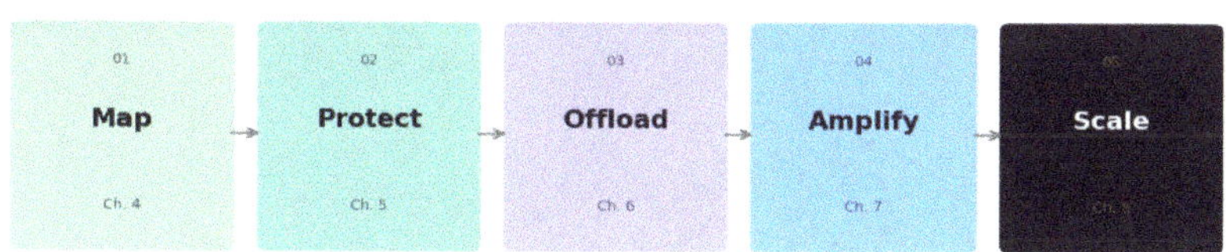

Figure 3 — The Amplification Framework: five stages from Map to Scale

CHAPTER

4

Know Your Terrain

PART II

> *"The significant problems we face cannot be solved at the same level of thinking we were at when we created them."*
> — Albert Einstein, as cited in Covey, S.R., The 7 Habits of Highly Effective People (1989), p. 42

The Navigation Imperative

A navigator who does not know their current position cannot plot a course to their destination, however clearly, they can envision it. This seems obvious when stated plainly, yet it describes with uncomfortable precision the situation of most professionals attempting to improve their working lives. They know, in a general sense, that they would like to spend more time on meaningful work and less time on administrative burden. What they lack is a precise, quantified, honest account of where they actually are today.

The Map stage of the Amplification Framework addresses this deficit. Its purpose is not to generate a plan, that comes later, but to generate an accurate picture of the current distribution of your professional time and energy across the full spectrum of task types. The precision of this picture will determine the effectiveness of everything that follows.

The Task Taxonomy

For the purposes of the mapping exercise, we employ a four-category taxonomy of professional tasks. This taxonomy is derived from the intersection of three analytical frameworks: the urgency-importance matrix popularized by President Dwight D. Eisenhower, Koch's 80/20 distribution analysis, and the Zone-of-Genius framework developed in Chapter Two.

Category One comprises Core Genius Work: tasks that directly deploy your Zone of Genius, the activities that require your unique combination of talent, expertise, and perspective, and that produce results far beyond the time invested. Category Two comprises Necessary Infrastructure: tasks that must be done to support your role but that do not require your unique genius, administrative tasks, routine communication, standard reporting, and procedural compliance. Category Three comprises Delegable Responsibilities: tasks that require the authority or organizational relationships of your position but that could, with appropriate briefing and oversight, be executed by someone else. Category Four comprises Automatable Processes: tasks that are rule-governed, repetitive, and data-driven, the natural candidates for AI-assisted or fully automated handling.

Building Your 20% Map

The construction of your 20% Map proceeds over two weeks. During this period, you maintain a time log, not a task list, but an honest accounting of how time is actually spent. The distinction is important: task lists record what you intended to do, while time logs record what you actually did.

Time-tracking tools such as Toggl, RescueTime, Harvest, and their equivalents can automate the data collection phase. The more analytically demanding phase is the categorization: for each recorded block of time, you must assign it to one of the four categories above with honesty and precision. This exercise is harder than it sounds, because many tasks have elements of multiple categories and because the categorization forces an honest reckoning with how much of your day is occupied by work that does not actually require you.

At the end of two weeks, calculate your Twenty Percent Ratio: the percentage of total working hours occupied by Category One activities. Research conducted across diverse professional populations suggests that the average knowledge worker's Twenty Percent Ratio is between eight and fifteen percent. Elite performers, those who have deliberately cultivated their Zone of Genius and protected it against displacement, typically report ratios of thirty to forty-five percent. The ambition of this book is to help you move from wherever you are today toward that latter range.

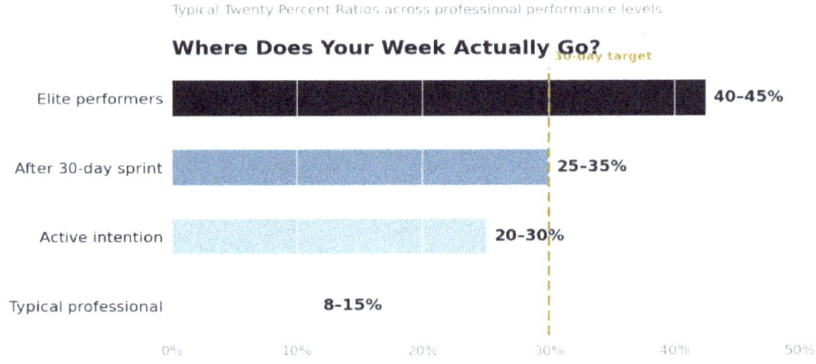

Figure 4 — Twenty Percent Ratios across professional performance levels

The Weekly 20% Ratio

In addition to the overall two-week mapping exercise, it is valuable to track a simpler weekly metric: the number of uninterrupted hours per week spent in Category One work. This weekly figure is the leading indicator most closely correlated with the long-term outcomes the Amplification Framework is designed to produce.

Harvard Business School researchers Teresa Amabile and Steven Kramer, in *The Progress Principle*, found that the single most powerful predictor of daily engagement and performance is making meaningful progress in meaningful work.

Not recognition. Not incentives. Not leadership inspiration. Progress — in work that matters to the person doing it.

> *"Of all the things that can boost emotions, motivation, and perceptions during a workday, the single most important is making progress in meaningful work."*
> — Teresa Amabile & Steven Kramer, The Progress Principle (2011), p. 3

You cannot protect what you have not mapped. Now that the map exists, Chapter Five builds the fortress around it.

AI PROMPT, Chapter 4

Use this prompt to categorize every task in your role and calculate your baseline Twenty Percent Ratio.

> *"Act as my productivity strategist. I am going to share all the recurring tasks and responsibilities in my role: [list them in detail]. Your task: categorize each one as (A) Core Genius Work requiring my unique capabilities, (B) Necessary Infrastructure that must be done but doesn't require my unique genius, (C) Delegable Responsibilities that need my authority but not my unique skills, or (D) Automatable Processes that are rule-governed and repetitive. After categorizing, identify: (1) My current approximate 20% Ratio, (2) The top three Category C or D tasks I should address first, and (3) One practical first step to begin the transition for each of those three tasks."*

Endnotes: Einstein, A. & Infeld, L. (1938). The Evolution of Physics. New York: Simon & Schuster, chapter opening quote. Senge, P. (1990). The Fifth Discipline. New York: Currency/Doubleday. Amabile, T. & Kramer, S. (2011). The Progress Principle. Boston: Harvard Business Review Press. Koch, R. (1997). The 80/20 Principle. London: Nicholas Brealey. Eisenhower Matrix: attribution to Dwight D. Eisenhower, popularized by Covey, S. (1989). The 7 Habits of Highly Effective People. New York: Free Press.

CHAPTER

5

Build Your Fortress

PART II

> *"The faculty of voluntarily bringing back a wandering attention, over and over again, is the very root of judgment, character, and will. An education which should improve this faculty would be the education par excellence."*
> — William James, The Principles of Psychology (1890), Vol. 1, p. 424

Why Intention Is Not Enough

The most common failure mode after the Map stage is this: professionals fully intend to protect their twenty percent, but they don't build the structures to make that intention durable against daily organizational pressure.

Intention without structure is just aspiration.

This insight is not merely practical wisdom; it is supported by decades of converging research in behavioral psychology. Behavioral scientist BJ Fogg, psychologist Peter Gollwitzer, and social psychologist Roy Baumeister have reached the same conclusion from different directions. People who maintain desired behaviors don't do it through superior willpower. They do it through superior design. They build environments where the right choice is the easy choice. They engineer their environments so that the desired behavior is the path of least resistance, and the undesired behavior requires deliberate effort to pursue.

Deep Work Architecture

Newport identifies four depth philosophies: Monastic (virtually all working time devoted to a single deep pursuit), Bimodal (alternating between deep and shallow work), Rhythmic (a fixed daily deep-work ritual), and Journalistic (inserting deep work whenever a gap allows).

For most professionals embedded in organizations, the Rhythmic philosophy is most viable. It means identifying a specific daily block — ideally two to four consecutive hours at your peak cognitive time — and defending it with the same seriousness as your most important client meeting.

The words 'defending that block' deserve emphasis. Research on sleep and cognitive performance — including work by UC Berkeley neuroscientist Matthew Walker and sleep researchers — demonstrates that peak cognitive hours, typically in the two to four hours following full wakefulness for most individuals, are genuinely scarce. They exist. They are finite. And they are, in the typical contemporary organization, routinely consumed by whatever demand presents itself first in the morning inbox.

The Meeting Budget

One of the most practical protective tools is the Meeting Budget: a weekly allocation of hours available for synchronous, unplanned, or low-genius activities, treated with the same discipline as a financial budget.

The logic is straightforward. If you have forty available working hours in a week and your Target Twenty Percent Ratio is thirty percent, then twelve hours must be protected for genuine genius work.

Those twelve hours are not available for meetings, email, or informal relationship-maintenance. The meeting budget is simply the numerical expression of that constraint.

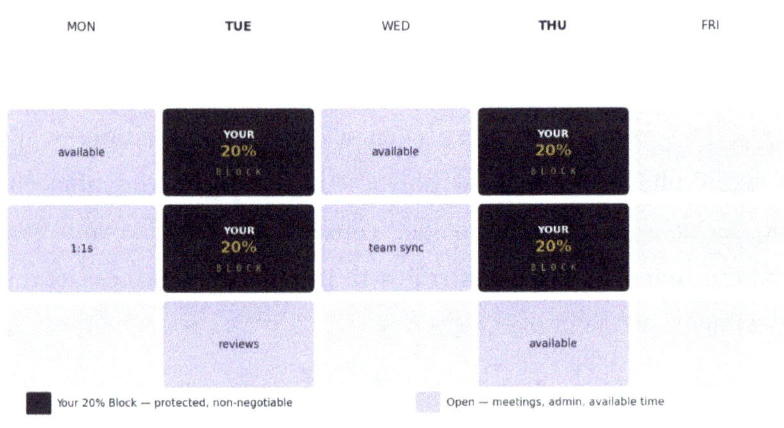

Figure 2 — The Fortress Calendar: Your 20% Blocks are non-negotiable

Scripts for Boundary Setting

The interpersonal dimension of protection, the ability to decline, redirect, and renegotiate requests without damaging professional relationships, is, for many high-performing professionals, the most challenging aspect of the Protect stage. The difficulty is partly psychological (the guilt and identity issues discussed in Chapter Three) and partly pragmatic: most professionals have not developed a repertoire of professional scripts for doing this gracefully.

Three scripts, derived from the work of William Ury and negotiation theory, are offered here as starting points. The first is the Graceful Redirect: 'I want to give this the attention it deserves. Let me look at my schedule and suggest a time when I can be fully present, or better yet, let me connect you with [colleague] who is working on exactly this type of problem.' The second is the Async Alternative: 'Rather than scheduling a meeting, could I send you a brief note with my thinking? I can often be more useful in writing than in a live discussion for this type of question.' The third is the Honest Accounting: 'I'm going to be direct with you, I have three major commitments this week that I've already committed to. Can we discuss which of those I should deprioritize to take this on?'

Protection without offloading is just a better-defended version of the same problem. Chapter Six is where the eighty percent finally starts to disappear.

AI AGENT, Chapter 5

Use this prompt as a weekly calendar guardian — it reviews your schedule and protects your most valuable hours before the week begins.

> *"You are my calendar guardian. Every Monday morning I will share my planned schedule for the week with you. Your ongoing mission: (1) Identify all blocks of genuine 20% Genius Work already protected; (2) Flag any meeting that could plausibly be handled asynchronously; (3) Identify any day with no protected deep work time; (4) Suggest a revised schedule that protects at least three 90-minute uninterrupted blocks for my core genius work. My current Zone of Genius is: [describe it]. My peak cognitive hours are: [specify]. Begin by reviewing this week's schedule: [paste schedule]."*

Endnotes: James, W. (1890). The Principles of Psychology, Vol. 1. New York: Henry Holt, chapter opening quote, p. 424. Newport, C. (2016). Deep Work. Grand Central Publishing. Fogg, B.J. (2019). Tiny Habits. Houghton Mifflin Harcourt. Gollwitzer, P. (1999). Implementation Intentions. American Psychologist, 54(7), 493–503. Baumeister, R. & Tierney, J. (2011). Willpower. New York: Penguin Press. Ury, W. (1991). Getting Past No. New York: Bantam. Huffington, A. (2016). The Sleep Revolution. New York: Harmony Books.

CHAPTER 6

Free Yourself From the 80%

PART II

> *"The first rule of any technology used in a business is that automation applied to an efficient operation will magnify the efficiency. The second is that automation applied to an inefficient operation will magnify the inefficiency."*
> — Bill Gates, Business @ the Speed of Thought (1999), p. 52

The Liberation Imperative

Protecting your twenty percent is necessary but insufficient. Protection creates the container; Offloading is what fills it with time freed from the eighty percent. To substantively increase the hours available for Zone of Genius work, you must actively offload the eighty percent, deliberately transferring tasks to other people, processes, and increasingly, to AI systems. This is the Offload stage, and it is where the greatest immediate gains in Twenty Percent Ratio are typically achieved.

The resistance to offloading is, paradoxically, strongest among the professionals who stand to benefit from it most. The expert who has mastered a domain is frequently the last person to delegate within that domain, because mastery creates both the capacity to do things faster than others and the identity investment in doing them personally. Yet it is precisely the expert's time, their Zone of Genius time, that is most costly to misallocate.

The Delegation Ladder

Not all delegation is equal. The most useful framework for thinking about levels of delegation is what we might call the Delegation Ladder, a five-level scale that describes the degree of independence granted to the person or system receiving the delegated task.

Rung One, at the lowest level of delegation, is Investigate and Report: the delegate researches the situation and reports the findings, but all decisions remain with the delegator. Rung Two is Recommend: the delegate researches and presents a recommendation but waits for approval before acting. Rung Three is Act and Report: the delegate takes action and informs the delegator after the fact. Rung Four is Act Autonomously within Parameters: the delegate handles the task completely within defined boundaries, informing the delegator only if those boundaries are exceeded. Rung Five is Full Ownership: the delegator is entirely removed from the loop.

The typical professional delegation failure occurs when a delegator attempts Rung Five delegation with a delegate only prepared for Rung Two. The result is predictable: the delegation fails, the manager concludes that delegation doesn't work, and the task lands back on their desk. The Delegation Ladder provides a framework for diagnosing the appropriate level of delegation for each task and each delegate at each point in time, and for incrementally moving delegated tasks up the ladder as the delegate's capability and trust develop.

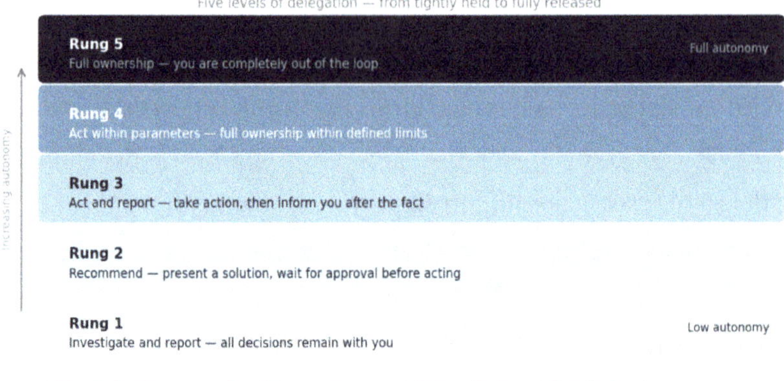

Figure 6 — The Delegation Ladder: five levels from investigate-and-report to full ownership

AI as Your 80% Assistant

The emergence of capable AI language models represents, for the first time in history, the availability of a truly unlimited eighty-percent assistant. The implications of this are significant and still being absorbed by most organizations and individuals. A human delegate needs time, context, and careful management. An AI assistant needs a well-designed prompt. That difference in overhead is where hours come from.

The key question for the Offload stage is: which of my Category Two, Three, and Four tasks — Necessary Infrastructure, Delegable Responsibilities, Pure Overhead — can be moved off my personal task list without meaningful loss of quality or control?

The Handoff Protocol

Whether delegating to a human or designing an AI prompt for a recurring task, the quality of your handoff is the primary determinant of output quality. This is obvious in principle and violated constantly in practice.

A well-designed handoff protocol specifies five elements: Context (what is the purpose and background of this task?), Inputs (what information, documents, or data are available?), Constraints (what limits, standards, or preferences must be respected?), Output Format (what should the deliverable look like?), and Success Criteria (how will we evaluate whether this was done well?). This five-element protocol applies equally to human delegation and AI prompting, a correspondence that is not accidental, since effective AI prompting is, at its core, a form of precision instruction.

Every task you have moved off your plate is an hour returned to your genius. Chapter Seven is about what to do with that time once you have it back.

AI PROMPT, Chapter 6

Use this prompt to design a complete handoff system for any recurring task you want off your plate permanently.

> *"I have a recurring task I currently handle every week that I want to systematically offload. The task is: [describe the task in detail, including context, typical inputs, and desired outputs]. Please help me design a complete handoff protocol by: (1) Writing a detailed Standard Operating Procedure (SOP) I could give to a team member or virtual assistant; (2) Identifying any components of this task that could be handled entirely by AI; (3) Writing the exact AI prompt(s) I would use for those AI-handled components; (4) Suggesting how I would audit quality once this task is off my direct plate. Be specific, practical, and thorough."*

Endnotes: Gates, B. (1999). Business @ the Speed of Thought. New York: Warner Books. Oncken, W. & Wass, D. (1974). Management Time: Who's Got the Monkey? Harvard Business Review, 52(6), 75–80. Blanchard, K., Zigarmi, P. & Zigarmi, D. (1985). Leadership and the One Minute Manager. New York: Morrow.

CHAPTER

7

Go Deeper Into Your Genius

PART II

> *"We are what we repeatedly do. Excellence, then, is not an act, but a habit."*
> — Will Durant, paraphrasing Aristotle's Nicomachean Ethics, in The Story of Philosophy (1926), p. 87. note: this precise formulation is Durant's synthesis, not a verbatim Aristotle translation

The Compounding Logic of Genius

The first three stages of the Amplification Framework, Map, Protect, and Offload, are primarily acts of recovery: recovering time and attention from the grip of the eighty percent. The Amplify stage is different in kind. It is not about recovery but about growth, about systematically deepening your Zone of Genius so that not only do you spend more time within it, but the quality of what you produce within it compounds over time.

Most frameworks focus on protecting time for genius work — which is necessary — but stop short of addressing what to do with that time once it has been protected.

The answer developed across Chapters Seven and Eight involves two interconnected practices: deliberate practice within your Zone of Genius, and strategic skill stacking around it.

Deliberate Practice Within Your Zone

Psychologist Anders Ericsson's research on deliberate practice, the mode of skill development most predictably associated with expert-level performance, offers the key principles for the Amplify stage.

Deliberate practice, as Ericsson defines it, is not merely practicing a skill repeatedly; it is engaging with a carefully designed sequence of challenges at the precise boundary of current capability, with immediate feedback and the explicit intent to improve specific sub-components of performance.

Applied to the twenty-percent context, deliberate practice means identifying the specific dimensions of your Zone of Genius work where you are good but not yet extraordinary, the precise capabilities within your genius domain that represent the frontier of your current development and designing regular practice activities that stretch those specific capabilities.

> *"The key to improving performance lies not in the amount of experience but in the way experience is transformed into improvement: through deliberate practice."*
> — Anders Ericsson & Robert Pool, Peak: Secrets from the New Science of Expertise (2016), p. 98

If you understand this principle, you don't simply do more genius work and expect improvement to follow automatically. You study your best work with the analytical eye of a coach, identifying what distinguished your finest outputs from your merely good ones, diagnosing the specific capabilities that made the difference, and designing deliberate practice activities to strengthen those capabilities further.

Strategic Skill Stacking

The concept of skill stacking, the strategic combination of multiple skills into a distinctive capability profile, was popularized by Scott

Adams, creator of the Dilbert comic strip, who described his own success as the product not of being the world's best cartoonist, nor the world's best writer, nor the world's best business observer, but of being unusually good at all three simultaneously. The combination, rather than any individual skill, was the source of distinctive value.

Within the Amplify framework, skill stacking is applied specifically within and around the Zone of Genius. The goal is not to accumulate skills broadly — it's to identify the three to five complementary capabilities that, combined with your core genius, create a profile no one else can replicate.

Depth is not enough on its own. Chapter Eight takes what you have built and asks a harder question: how do you make it bigger than yourself?

AI PROMPT, Chapter 7

Use this prompt to build a 90-day deliberate practice plan for going deeper into the work only you can do.

> *"My Zone of Genius, as I currently understand it, is: [describe in detail]. I want to go significantly deeper in this area over the next 90 days. Please design a specific Deliberate Practice Roadmap for me, including: (1) The 3 most important sub-capabilities within my zone that I should develop to become truly extraordinary; (2) Specific practice activities I can do within my actual work to develop each capability; (3) How I should measure and track progress each week; (4) Suggested reading, study, or exposure that would accelerate development in this area; (5) One person in my professional network who likely has deep expertise in this zone and with whom I should seek a deeper mentoring relationship."*

Endnotes: Ericsson, A. & Pool, R. (2016). Peak. Eamon Dolan/Houghton Mifflin Harcourt. Adams, S. (2013). How to Fail at Almost Everything and Still Win Big. New York: Portfolio/Penguin. Durant, W. (1926). The Story of Philosophy. New York: Simon & Schuster.

CHAPTER 8

Multiply Your 20% Beyond Yourself

PART II

> *"The whole is greater than the sum of its parts."*
> — Aristotle, Metaphysics, Book H, 1045a.8–10

From Personal Practice to Organizational Reach

The four stages examined in the preceding chapters, Map, Protect, Offload, and Amplify, have been primarily concerned with your individual experience of work. The Scale stage shifts the unit of analysis from the individual to the team and, ultimately, to the organization. It asks: once you have identified and deepened your Zone of Genius, how can you create systems and structures that multiply its impact beyond the limits of your own personal output?

The Scale stage is the one most commonly neglected in personal-productivity frameworks. Yet it is arguably the stage with the greatest leverage: a professional who has found ways to systematize and teach their genius creates an organization-wide capability multiplier.

Knowledge Transfer: Multiplying Your Impact

The first scaling mechanism is deliberate knowledge transfer: converting tacit knowledge, the intuitive expertise in your Zone of Genius, into explicit knowledge that others can learn from, apply, and build upon. This is a non-trivial challenge. Research in knowledge management, dating from Ikujiro Nonaka and Hirotaka Takeuchi's landmark 1995 work The Knowledge-Creating Company, has consistently found that the most valuable organizational knowledge is the hardest to codify: it resides in the judgments, heuristics, and pattern recognition capacities of expert practitioners, and resists capture in standard documentation formats.

The solution Nonaka and Takeuchi propose, the process of "externalization" — putting implicit expertise into words, diagrams, and examples that others can learn from — maps closely onto the practical techniques available to anyone seeking to scale their genius. Regular case discussions with team members, documented decision rationales, annotated examples of your best work, and structured reflection on what distinguished your excellent outputs from your merely good ones all serve the externalization purpose.

> *"Knowledge is created only by individuals. An organization cannot create knowledge without individuals. The organization supports creative individuals or provides contexts for them to create knowledge."*
>
> — Ikujiro Nonaka & Hirotaka Takeuchi, The Knowledge-Creating Company (1995), p. 239

Building a 20% Culture

The most ambitious application of the Scale stage is the construction of a team or organizational culture in which every member is enabled and encouraged to identify, protect, and develop their own Zone of Genius. This requires the leader to move beyond optimizing their own twenty percent and to actively work to remove the structural barriers that prevent others from doing the same.

Amy Edmondson's research at Harvard Business School shows that psychological safety changes what people bring to their work. When people believe it's safe to take interpersonal risks, they share their most creative, unguarded thinking. When they don't, you get the safe version. A twenty-percent culture is, by definition, a psychologically safe culture: one in which the organization's interest is visibly invested in the full expression of each person's distinctive capabilities, rather than in the management of conformity to standard expectations.

You have mapped, protected, offloaded, amplified, and scaled. The framework is complete. Part Three introduces the force multiplier that can accelerate every stage of it.

AI PROMPT, Chapter 8

Use this prompt to design a knowledge transfer system that lets your team access your expertise without needing you in the room.

> *"I want to systematically scale my expertise in [your Zone of Genius] so that my team can access and apply it without being entirely dependent on my direct involvement. Help me design a Knowledge Transfer System by specifying: (1) The three most important dimensions of my expertise that I should document first, including how to structure that documentation for practical usefulness; (2) A simple teaching format I could use to share this knowledge with my team regularly (e.g., weekly case reviews, annotated examples, structured coaching conversations); (3) How AI tools could help my team access my expertise asynchronously, for example, through a custom AI assistant trained on my approaches and principles; (4) How I would know, within 90 days, whether the knowledge transfer is working."*

Endnotes: Aristotle. Metaphysics. Trans. W.D. Ross. Book H, 1045a.8–10. Oxford: Clarendon Press, 1924. Nonaka, I. & Takeuchi, H. (1995). The Knowledge-Creating Company. New York: Oxford University Press. Edmondson, A.C. (1999). Psychological Safety and Learning Behavior in Work Teams. Administrative Science Quarterly, 44(2), 350–383, for the foundational team safety research cited in this chapter; for the organizational application, see Edmondson, A.C. (2018). The Fearless Organization. Hoboken: Wiley.

PART III

AI as Your 20% Multiplier

Artificial intelligence represents the most significant structural change in the economics of knowledge work since the personal computer. But its relevance to the twenty-percent framework is specific and must be understood precisely: AI is not a substitute for human genius, but it is an extraordinarily capable substitute for the eighty percent of work that surrounds and suppresses that genius. The four chapters in this section provide both the philosophical framework and the practical toolkit for deploying AI as a systematic twenty-percent multiplier.

CHAPTER

9

Rethinking AI: Your 80% Slayer

PART III

> *"The real danger is not that computers will begin to think like men, but that men will begin to think like computers."*
> — Sydney J. Harris, Clearing the Ground (1986)

The Misuse of Transformative Technology

A few years ago I worked with a client who had convinced themselves they had cracked the AI problem. The pitch to their C-Suite was clean and compelling: deploy agentic AI workflows — autonomous systems that act independently without constant human input — across the customer service function, reduce headcount, shrink the expense line, show investors a leaner operation. On paper, it looked like exactly what boards want to see. Efficiency. Scale. Innovation.

The reality was more complicated. And more costly.

What they were actually doing was removing the humans from the part of their business where customers were already most frustrated. They weren't automating paperwork or internal reporting or compliance documentation, the genuinely repetitive work no one values. They were automating the relationship. They built a paywall around real human support. They made it structurally difficult for customers to reach a person.

The data came back fast. Customer satisfaction dropped. Social media filled with complaints. Churn increased in segments that had historically been their most loyal. The story in the press wasn't 'innovative company streamlines operations.' It was 'company abandons its customers.'

Within months, they were rehiring. Not because AI had failed them. Because they had asked AI to do the wrong job. They had used it to eliminate the human contact their customers actually needed, while leaving untouched the mountains of internal process work that genuinely could have been automated without any customer ever noticing.

Here's what I've watched play out across every sector I've worked in: companies under investor pressure to show growth will reach for AI as a cost-cutting mechanism before they reach for it as a capability multiplier. It's the faster, more legible move. You can put a number on headcount reduction in a quarterly report. You can't easily put a number on what your best people could accomplish if you freed them from the work that doesn't need them.

The irony is sharp. The same companies laying off customer service teams to fund AI investments are the ones that haven't yet automated the internal work that genuinely could disappear tomorrow without anyone missing it. The eighty percent is still sitting there. Untouched. While the twenty percent, the human judgment, the relationship, the trust, gets handed to a bot.

Faster execution of the wrong decision is still the wrong decision.

Throughout history, transformative technologies have first been used to do faster what was already being done — rather than to reimagine what should be done at all. The printing press reproduced manuscripts. The automobile was a horseless carriage. The internet was a faster postal service.

In each case, the technology's real potential was only realized when the question shifted from 'how do I do this faster?' to 'what becomes possible now that wasn't before?'

Artificial intelligence, in the current professional landscape, is being deployed predominantly in the first mode: as a way to do familiar tasks faster. Professionals use AI to draft emails more quickly, to produce first drafts of reports with less initial effort, to generate meeting summaries with less manual effort. These are useful applications. They're not, however, the application that will produce the magnitude of change available to those willing to ask the deeper question.

The deeper question, and the one this chapter is designed to help you ask, is this: which of the tasks currently occupying my eighty percent can be transferred so completely to AI systems that they require no meaningful human time investment? Not 'how can AI help me do these tasks faster?' but 'how can AI make these tasks disappear from my schedule entirely?'

What AI Can and Cannot Replace

To deploy AI intelligently in the twenty-percent framework, we must be analytically precise about the domains in which current AI capabilities are strong and those in which they are genuinely weak. Confusing these is both a strategic error and a potentially costly one.

Current large language models excel at tasks that are primarily language-based and that benefit from synthesis, drafting, and pattern recognition across large bodies of text: drafting communications and documents; summarizing complex materials; generating structured first drafts; conducting background research; creating templates and frameworks; translating between technical and non-technical registers; generating variations on existing content; and applying rule-governed processes to new inputs.

Current AI systems are significantly less reliable at tasks requiring: genuine novel insight grounded in embodied experience; carefully considered emotional intelligence in high-stakes interpersonal situations; ethical judgment in complex, context-dependent situations; original creative synthesis that draws on deeply personal accumulated experience; and strategic judgment that depends on tacit knowledge of a specific organizational context.

This mapping AI's strengths aligning closely with the eighty percent, AI's weaknesses aligning closely with the twenty percent — is not coincidental. AI excels at tasks that are language-based, pattern-driven, and replicable, which describes most of the eighty percent. It struggles with tasks requiring original judgment, embodied experience, and contextual intuition, which describes most of the twenty percent.

> *"We know more than we can tell."*
> — Michael Polanyi, The Tacit Dimension (1966), p. 4

The Five Categories of AI-Offloadable Work

Based on an analysis of current AI capabilities and the task taxonomy developed in Chapter Four, five categories of work are most amenable to substantial AI offloading: Information Processing (reading, synthesizing, and extracting key insights from documents, reports, and communications); Communication Drafting (producing first drafts of emails, reports, proposals, and presentations); Research and Analysis (gathering, organizing, and presenting background information on any topic); Administrative Coordination (scheduling, agenda preparation, meeting summarization, and action-item tracking); and Process Execution (applying defined rules and procedures to new inputs to generate consistent, standardized outputs).

In the typical professional's workweek, these five categories account for between thirty-five and fifty-five percent of total working time. The potential recovery, if even half of this time were genuinely transferred to AI systems, is significant: seven to eleven hours per week available for reallocation to Zone of Genius work.

The question is no longer whether AI can help. It is whether you are using it on the right things. Chapter Ten builds the daily system that makes that happen automatically.

AI SETUP PROMPT, Chapter 9

Use this prompt to set up AI as your personal Chief of Staff — one that filters every task through a single question: does this actually need you?

> *"You are my personal AI Chief of Staff. Your ongoing mission is to help me spend as much of my working time as possible in my Zone of Genius, which I define as: [describe your 20%]. Every time I bring you a task, your first diagnostic question should be: 'Does this task actually require your unique expertise and judgment?' If the honest answer is no, your job is to handle it yourself, delegate it to someone else, or design a system so it is handled automatically in the future. Begin by asking me five questions that will help you understand my role, my priorities, and my working style deeply enough to serve this mission effectively."*

Endnotes: Polanyi, M. (1966). The Tacit Dimension. New York: Doubleday. Harris, S.J. (1986). Clearing the Ground. Boston: Houghton Mifflin. Brynjolfsson, E. & McAfee, A. (2014). The Second Machine Age. New York: Norton. Autor, D. (2015). Why Are There Still So Many Jobs? Journal of Economic Perspectives, 29(3), 3–30.

CHAPTER

10

Building Your AI Workflow Stack

PART III

> *"Systems thinking is a discipline for seeing wholes. It is a framework for seeing interrelationships rather than things, for seeing patterns of change rather than static snapshots."*
>
> — Peter Senge, The Fifth Discipline (1990), p. 73

From Individual Prompts to Integrated Systems

The professionals who derive the greatest ongoing benefit from AI tools are not those who use AI for occasional ad hoc tasks when the need arises. They are those who have built structured, repeatable workflows, systems in which AI is a regular, anticipated component of the daily and weekly cycle, taking over specific categories of work with sufficient reliability and quality that they have genuinely removed those categories from their cognitive agenda.

The distinction is analogous to the difference between occasionally asking a talented colleague for help and hiring a full-time staff member. The former is useful but occasional; the latter creates structural capacity. Building an AI Workflow Stack is the process of creating that structural capacity, designing a set of AI-powered routines that reliably handle defined portions of your eighty percent, every day, without requiring your active involvement.

The Morning Ritual

The highest-value component of an AI Workflow Stack is the Morning Ritual, a structured interaction with an AI system at the beginning of each working day, before the demands of the day have begun to pull at your attention. The purpose of the Morning Ritual is threefold: to clarify your priorities for the day, to identify and delegate to AI the tasks that do not require your personal attention, and to enter your first period of deep work with a clear agenda and a reduced cognitive load.

A well-designed Morning Ritual prompt takes approximately three to five minutes to complete and generates an output that includes: confirmation of the day's top priorities, a suggested schedule for the day that protects your peak cognitive hours for Category One work, a list of communications or tasks that AI can handle on your behalf, and identification of any incoming requests or information that require your specific attention before the day begins.

The AI Triage System

The second component of the AI Workflow Stack is the Triage System, a protocol for handling the continuous stream of incoming requests, emails, and tasks in a way that ensures your personal attention is reserved for items that actually require it. The design of an effective AI Triage System requires three elements: a classification scheme (how incoming items are categorized according to what type of response they require), a routing protocol (which categories are handled by AI, which are escalated to you, and which are delegated to team members), and quality standards (what constitutes an acceptable AI-handled response for each category).

The development of an effective triage system typically takes two to three weeks of iterative refinement. During the first week, the professional monitors the AI's handling of classified items and corrects misclassifications and substandard responses. By week three, a well-designed triage system can handle the majority of routine incoming items without requiring significant human attention — freeing focused review for the items that genuinely need it.

The Weekly AI Review

The third component of the stack is the Weekly Review, a regular, structured session in which you use AI assistance to analyze the past week's work, identify patterns and opportunities, and design the following week's schedule for maximum Twenty Percent Ratio.

The Weekly Review is arguably the highest-value use of AI in the entire twenty-percent framework. It is the moment at which the system turns back on itself, in which AI helps you analyze how well you are deploying your own AI-assisted offloading, identify the remaining inefficiencies in your current workflow, and progressively refine the system toward higher performance.

A workflow without a prompt strategy is an engine without fuel. Chapter Eleven gives you the language to ask AI for precisely what you need.

MORNING RITUAL PROMPT, Chapter 10

Use this prompt every morning to start the day with clarity, offload what AI can handle, and protect your best hours before demands arrive.

> *"Good morning. I want to begin this day well. Here are the three most important outcomes I need to achieve today: [list them]. Here is everything else currently on my task list and in my inbox: [list or describe]. Please: (1) Confirm which of my task list items align directly with my top 3 outcomes; (2) Suggest which items you can handle or draft on my behalf with no further input from me, and write a first draft for each of those now; (3) Identify any items that should be delegated and to whom; (4) Flag anything that requires my personal attention before my first deep work session at [time]; (5) Suggest a time-blocked schedule for today that protects at least [X] hours for my top 3 priorities."*

Endnotes: Senge, P. (1990). The Fifth Discipline. New York: Currency/Doubleday. Allen, D. (2001). Getting Things Done. New York: Viking. Newport, C. (2016). Deep Work. Grand Central Publishing.

CHAPTER

11

Prompt Design for 20% Thinkers

PART III

> *"The formulation of a problem is often more essential than its solution, which may be merely a matter of mathematical or experimental skill."*
> — Albert Einstein & Leopold Infeld, The Evolution of Physics (1938), p. 92

The Architecture of Effective Prompting

The quality of output you receive from an AI system is, in almost all cases, a direct function of the quality of input you provide. This sounds obvious — and is violated constantly in practice.

Most people approach AI tools with the same vague, context-free requests they'd type into a search engine: "write me an email," "summarize this document," "give me some ideas." The results are correspondingly generic.

The mastery of prompt design is therefore not a technical skill in the conventional sense; it does not require programming knowledge or technical expertise. It is, rather, a discipline of precision specification: the ability to translate one's intent, context, constraints, and expectations into a form that enables the AI system to generate outputs of genuinely useful quality.

The SCOPE Framework

The SCOPE framework provides a structured approach to prompt design that has proven effective across a wide range of professional contexts. SCOPE is an acronym for five elements: Situation, Context, Output, Parameters, and Examples.

Situation specifies the role and relationship you wish to establish with the AI for this interaction: 'You are a strategic communications expert reviewing a proposal for a major client.' Context provides the background information the AI needs to generate an appropriate response: relevant history, constraints, stakeholder information, and the problem being addressed. Output specifies precisely what form the response should take: 'Provide a three-paragraph executive summary followed by a bulleted list of five specific recommendations, in language appropriate for a non-specialist audience.' Parameters specify the constraints the response must respect: length, tone, format, level of technicality, and any topics to avoid. Examples, the most powerful and most underused element of the SCOPE framework, provide one or two examples of the type of output sought, which anchor the AI's pattern-completion to a concrete target.

Prompting as Thinking

One of the most valuable and least discussed uses of AI prompting in the twenty-percent framework is as a tool for thought, a means by which you can use the AI's responses to clarify, challenge, and develop your own thinking, rather than simply to produce outputs.

The Socratic function of well-designed AI prompting is surprisingly powerful. When wrestling with a strategic decision, you can structure an interaction with an AI system that forces you to articulate your assumptions, identify the weakest elements of your reasoning, consider perspectives you have not yet examined, and test your conclusions against challenging counterarguments. The AI is not generating the insight in these interactions. You are. The AI is providing the conversational structure that accelerates and sharpens it.

> *"Thinking is not the application of rules. It is the engagement with problems. And problems yield to engagement, not to formulas."*
> — Philosopher and educator John Dewey, How We Think (1910), p. 12

Building Your Personal Prompt Library

The professional who uses AI tools effectively does not generate fresh prompts from scratch for every interaction. They maintain a Personal Prompt Library: a curated collection of high-quality, role-specific prompts for their most common high-value interactions, organized for easy retrieval and rapid customization.

The construction of a Personal Prompt Library is a significant initial investment that pays sustained dividends. The library is built iteratively: as each prompt is used, it is refined based on the quality of the output it generates, and the most effective versions are retained as templates for future use. Over time, the library evolves into a systematic capture of the professional's most effective AI interaction patterns.

You can now design prompts that think with you. Chapter Twelve takes the next step: building agents that work for you while you are doing something else entirely.

META-PROMPT, Chapter 11

Use this prompt to build a personal library of reusable AI templates tailored to the five tasks you do most often.

> *"I want to build a Personal Prompt Library for my role as [your title/role]. My five most frequent high-value tasks are: [list them]. For each task, please write a reusable, high-quality prompt template using the SCOPE framework. Each template should: (1) Establish the appropriate AI role and relationship; (2) Include placeholders in [brackets] for the variable information I will fill in each time; (3) Specify the exact output format that would be most useful to me; (4) Include any standing constraints or preferences that apply to this type of work; (5) Reflect my professional voice and standards. Please write a complete template for each of the five tasks."*

Endnotes: Einstein, A. & Infeld, L. (1938). The Evolution of Physics. New York: Simon & Schuster, chapter opening quote, p. 92. Dewey, J. (1910). How We Think. Boston: D.C. Heath & Co. White, J. et al. (2023). A Prompt Pattern Catalog to Enhance Prompt Engineering with ChatGPT. arXiv:2302.11382. Zamfirescu-Pereira, J.D. et al. (2023). Why Johnny Can't Prompt: How Non-AI Experts Fail to Anticipate LLM Failures. CHI 2023.

CHAPTER

12

AI Agents: Your Always-On 80% Team

PART III

> *"The goal of automation is to remove all the friction from everything that doesn't matter, so that you have maximum friction-free access to the things that do."*
> — Kevin Kelly, The Inevitable (2016), p. 51

Beyond the Chatbot Model

Most professionals' experience with AI tools operates within the chatbot model: a human initiates a conversation, the AI responds, the human reviews the response and either uses it or continues the conversation. This is a powerful mode of interaction, and the preceding chapters have been primarily concerned with how to make it as effective as possible. But it is not the only mode available, and for certain categories of recurring work, it is not the most effective one.

AI agents, autonomous systems that are given a goal, provided with appropriate tools and information, and enabled to take sequences of actions over time without requiring human initiation of each step, represent a qualitatively different type of AI deployment. Where the chatbot model positions AI as a responsive tool, the agent model positions AI as a proactive team member: one that operates continuously on defined tasks, handles defined workflows, and escalates to human judgment only when the task exceeds its defined scope.

Five Agent Types for the Knowledge Worker

Five types of AI agents are most immediately valuable for the knowledge worker seeking to offload recurring eighty-percent tasks.

The first is the Communication Manager agent, which monitors incoming communications, classifies them by type and priority, drafts responses for low-priority items, and surfaces high-priority items with appropriate context for human review. The second is the Research Synthesizer agent, which monitors defined information sources, identifies items relevant to the professional's areas of concern, and produces regular briefings synthesizing key developments.

The third is the Meeting Preparation agent, which, given access to calendar information and relevant background documents, automatically prepares meeting agendas, gathers relevant background materials, and generates post-meeting summaries and action items. The fourth is the Document Production agent, which maintains templates for recurring document types and, given structured inputs, produces complete first drafts requiring only review and refinement before use. The fifth is the Analytics and Reporting agent, which, given access to relevant data sources, automatically produces regular analytical reports according to predefined formats and distributes them to appropriate stakeholders.

Deploying Your First Agent

The deployment of a first AI agent need not be a technically complex undertaking. Modern AI platforms provide frameworks for building agent workflows at levels of technical complexity ranging from the simple (prompt sequences that retain context across interactions) to the sophisticated (fully automated multi-tool agents with complex branching logic). For the non-technical professional, beginning with the simpler end of this spectrum is advisable.

A practical first agent deployment begins with identifying a single recurring task, one that is time-consuming, well-defined, and currently handled manually, and designing a structured prompt sequence that handles that task end-to-end, with a human review step before final output. The professional runs this sequence manually several times, refining the prompts based on output quality. Once the sequence reliably produces output of acceptable quality, it can be formalized and, over time, more fully automated.

Your personal system is built. Part Four asks what happens when you bring this thinking into the room with the people you lead.

AGENT DESIGN PROMPT, Chapter 12

Use this prompt to design an AI agent that handles a specific recurring task automatically, without you in the loop.

> *"I want to design an AI agent that handles [describe the specific recurring task, e.g., 'preparing my weekly status report for leadership'] automatically. The task currently takes me approximately [X] hours per week. Please help me design this agent by specifying: (1) Exactly what information inputs the agent needs to do this task well; (2) A step-by-step workflow the agent should follow; (3) What decisions the agent should make autonomously versus escalate to me; (4) What the agent's outputs should look like, including a sample output template; (5) How I would measure the agent's performance quality; (6) What tools or data integrations the agent would need. Be as specific and practical as possible."*

Endnotes: Kelly, K. (2016). The Inevitable: Understanding the 12 Technological Forces That Will Shape Our Future. New York: Viking. Weng, L. (2023). LLM-powered Autonomous Agents. lilianweng.github.io. Russell, S. & Norvig, P. (2021). Artificial Intelligence: A Modern Approach (4th ed.). Pearson.

PART IV

The 20% Life, Beyond Work

The twenty-percent principle is not a productivity hack. It is a philosophy of human flourishing, one that asserts the deep moral seriousness of spending one's finite time on earth in activities that call forth one's highest capacities, rather than merely occupying one's hours with the fulfillment of others' expectations. The three chapters in this section extend the framework beyond the individual contributor to the leader, the career architect, and the whole person.

CHAPTER

13

The 20% Leader

PART IV

> *"The task of the leader is to get people from where they are to where they have not been."*
> — Henry Kissinger, Leadership: Six Studies in World Strategy (2022), p. xvii

Leading Genius, Not Just Managing Performance

Applying the twenty-percent framework at the leadership level requires a fundamental shift in how leaders understand their primary responsibility.

The conventional model — leader as task-completion overseer — isn't wrong, but it's incomplete. The twenty-percent leader's primary responsibility is not task management. It's capability deployment: ensuring each team member spends the maximum possible proportion of their time in their individual Zone of Genius.

This is both a moral commitment and a strategic one. The moral dimension is straightforward: people experience work as meaningful when it calls on their highest capacities. A leader who keeps assigning talented people to work that doesn't require their talent is, in a real sense, failing them. The strategic dimension is equally clear: the organization that systematically deploys its human capital at its Zone-of-Genius level will consistently outperform the organization that deploys talented people on work they don't need to be talented to do.

Mapping the Team's Collective Genius

The first leadership application of the twenty-percent framework is the construction of a Team Genius Map, a visual representation of the Zone of Genius of each team member and the degree to which current task allocations align with those zones. This exercise typically begins with one-on-one conversations in which the leader uses the diagnostic questions from Chapter Two to identify each team member's Zone of Genius, supplemented by their own observations of when each person operates at their highest level.

The Team Genius Map frequently reveals striking misallocations invisible in conventional performance management. The analyst spending sixty percent of their time on data entry and report formatting, when their genius lies in interpretive insight, is invisible in a dashboard that shows them as 'on track' against their deliverable targets. The leader who builds a Team Genius Map begins to see their team's work through a different lens: not 'is the work being done?' but 'is it being done by the person best positioned to do it at a genius level?'

The Leader as 80% Remover

Management consultant Patrick Lencioni's *Five Dysfunctions of a Team* documents how organizational dysfunction creates friction that impedes performance. From a twenty-percent perspective, the most damaging dysfunction is the absence of trust.

Not interpersonal trust — but the deeper professional trust that allows someone to say, without political consequence, that they are spending most of their time on work that doesn't require their best.

> *"Great leaders are almost always great simplifiers, who can cut through argument, debate and doubt to offer a solution everybody can understand."*
> — General Colin Powell, as cited in Harari, O. (2002). The Leadership Secrets of Colin Powell. McGraw-Hill, p. 164

The leader who clears the eighty percent for their team changes what the team is capable of. Chapter Fourteen asks what it means to do the same for your own career.

LEADERSHIP PROMPT, Chapter 13

Use this prompt to map your team's collective genius and build a 90-day plan for moving everyone closer to their best work.

> *"I manage a team of [N] people across [describe the team's function]. I want to help each person spend more time in their Zone of Genius. Please help me design: (1) A complete 1:1 conversation framework, specific questions I can use with each team member to discover their individual Zone of Genius and identify where their current role aligns or conflicts with it; (2) A simple visual format for capturing and sharing the Team Genius Map; (3) A practical 90-day plan for progressively restructuring task allocation so that each team member's highest-genius activities are protected and their lowest-genius activities are delegated or automated; (4) Metrics I could track to measure whether the team's overall Twenty Percent Ratio is improving over time."*

Endnotes: Lencioni, P. (2002). The Five Dysfunctions of a Team. San Francisco: Jossey-Bass. Edmondson, A. (2018). The Fearless Organization. Hoboken: Wiley. Kissinger, H. (2022). Leadership: Six Studies in World Strategy. New York: Penguin Press.

CHAPTER

14

The 20% Career

PART IV

> *"The most difficult thing is the decision to act. The rest is merely tenacity."*
> — Amelia Earhart, as cited in Butler, S. (2009). East to the Dawn. Da Capo Press, p. 308

The Promotion Trap

One of professional life's great structural ironies: the reward for excellent work in your Zone of Genius is frequently promotion to a role that requires you to spend less time there.

The exceptional individual contributor becomes a manager consumed by administrative oversight. The great front-line manager becomes a director buried in strategy meetings rather than the team development work at which they excelled.

This is so common it has its own name: the *Peter Principle*, articulated by Laurence J. Peter and Raymond Hull in 1969.

In hierarchical organizations, people are promoted based on performance in their current role — until they reach the level at which they are no longer competent. There they remain.

The implication is direct and practical: the twenty-percent career framework requires that professionals evaluate career opportunities not only according to conventional criteria (salary, title, organizational status, scope of responsibility) but explicitly according to their likely effect on the Twenty Percent Ratio. Will this new role give me more or less time in my Zone of Genius? Is the increased responsibility worth the increased distance from my highest-contribution work?

Making Your Genius Visible

One of the pragmatic challenges of a twenty-percent career strategy is that Zone of Genius work is often invisible to organizational decision-makers. The executive who spends two hours in a deeply focused state generating a breakthrough insight, and twenty minutes writing it up, may receive less organizational visibility than the colleague who attends twelve meetings per day and is consequently seen everywhere, by everyone, perpetually busy and engaged.

You must become deliberate about making your genius visible. This is not a call to self-promotion in the conventional sense; it is a recognition that organizational decision-makers allocate resources, including the resource of professional latitude, based on their understanding of who creates value and how. The person whose genius is invisible will not receive the organizational protection that genius work requires.

Strategies for making genius visible include: producing written artifacts from Zone of Genius work that can circulate beyond the immediate team (brief analyses, synthesis documents, strategic memos); speaking credibly and specifically in senior forums about the insights generated in deep work; developing a small number of high-visibility organizational relationships with leaders who understand and value what you do at your best; and deliberately connecting your twenty-percent outputs to organizational outcomes that leadership cares about.

Negotiating Your Zone

As professionals develop a clearer and more confident understanding of their Zone of Genius, they frequently discover that their current role, as formally defined, imposes unnecessary constraints on the time available for genius work that could be restructured through negotiation. Most professionals underestimate the degree to which their role definition is malleable, particularly when they can make a credible case that restructuring would increase their contribution to organizational outcomes.

The negotiation of role design is most effective when framed in organizational terms rather than personal ones. Not 'I would prefer to spend more time on strategic work,' but 'here is an analysis of where my time is currently allocated and where the data suggests I create the most outsized value, and here is a proposal for how we could restructure my responsibilities to increase that value by approximately X percent.'

Your career is a system. It can be redesigned. Chapter Fifteen widens the lens one final time, from career to life.

CAREER DESIGN PROMPT, Chapter 14

Use this prompt to analyze your career through the twenty percent lens and design a path toward a role where your genius is the point.

> *"I want to design a career trajectory that moves me progressively toward spending at least 50% of my working time in my Zone of Genius over the next three years. My Zone of Genius is: [describe it in detail]. My current role is: [describe it]. My current Twenty Percent Ratio is approximately: [X%]. Please help me: (1) Analyze the gap between my current role and my twenty-percent ideal; (2) Identify 3–5 possible career moves, including lateral moves, role redefinition, and conventional promotion paths, that would increase my genius ratio; (3) Develop a case I could make to my current leadership for restructuring my role to better align with my genius; (4) Identify specific steps I could take in the next 90 days to make my Zone of Genius more visible to organizational decision-makers."*

Endnotes: Peter, L. & Hull, R. (1969). The Peter Principle. New York: William Morrow. Pink, D. (2009). Drive: The Surprising Truth About What Motivates Us. New York: Riverhead. Ibarra, H. (2003). Working Identity: Unconventional Strategies for Reinventing Your Career. Boston: Harvard Business School Press.

CHAPTER

15

The 20% Life

PART IV

> *"The mass of men lead lives of quiet desperation. What is called resignation is confirmed desperation."*
> — Henry David Thoreau, Walden (1854), p. 8

Beyond Professional Optimization

This book has been primarily concerned with the application of the twenty-percent principle to professional life. But the principle is not, at its core, a professional one; it is a human one. The Zone of Genius is not a work concept; it is a life concept, the domain in which your deepest capacities, your most authentic values, and your most meaningful contributions converge. That domain does not disappear when you close your laptop at the end of the working day.

The most thoughtful applications of the twenty-percent principle extend it to the full canvas of a life: to personal relationships, to creative and intellectual pursuits, to physical health and embodied experience, to the commitments and obligations that constitute one's sense of responsibility to others. The question in each domain is the same: where are you operating in your Zone of Genius, and where are you allowing the eighty percent to crowd it out?

The Life Audit

The most comprehensive version of the twenty-percent diagnostic is a Full-Life Audit: an extension of the Calendar Autopsy from Chapter Three to encompass every significant domain of life. In each domain, professional work, primary relationships, health and physical life, creative and intellectual pursuits, community and service, leisure and restoration, the professional examines the ratio of time spent in activities that genuinely call upon their highest capacities and deepest values versus time spent in the habitual, the obligatory, and the merely comfortable.

The results of a Full-Life Audit are typically both illuminating and uncomfortable. You may have spent years developing a clear understanding of your Zone of Genius at work, only to discover that in your personal life you have been following patterns set years ago without ever questioning them. The relationships you maintain, the leisure activities you pursue, the community roles you occupy — many of these may reflect the accumulated weight of habit and obligation rather than deliberate choices about where your time creates the most meaning and value.

Time as the Fundamental Constraint

The fundamental premise of the twenty-percent principle, applied to life rather than merely to work, is the recognition of time as an absolutely finite resource. The psychologist Barry Schwartz, in *The Paradox of Choice*, observes that the expansion of options in modern life, while experienced as freedom, frequently produces paralysis and dissatisfaction, because the multiplication of choices increases the opportunity cost of any single choice and thereby makes it harder to invest fully in the path chosen.

The twenty-percent life is, in one sense, a practice of deliberate constraint: a willingness to say no to the good to say yes to the extraordinary. This is not a counsel of austerity or isolation; it is a counsel of intentionality. The full life, in the twenty-percent philosophy, is not the life that contains the most activities, relationships, and commitments, it is the life in which the activities, relationships, and commitments present are those that most fully call forth the best the person has to offer.

> *"Tell me, what is it you plan to do with your one wild and precious life?"*
>
> — Mary Oliver, "The Summer Day," New and Selected Poems (1992), p. 94

The twenty percent principle does not end when you close your laptop. Part Five is your thirty-day plan for making all of this real, starting now.

LIFE DESIGN PROMPT, Chapter 15

Use this prompt to apply the 80/20 principle to your whole life — not just your work — and protect what matters most.

> *"I want to apply the 80/20 principle to my whole life, not just my work. My core personal values are: [list 3–5]. The activities, relationships, and pursuits in my personal life that genuinely call upon my deepest capacities and create the most meaning are: [list them]. The obligations, habits, and time commitments in my personal life that feel like 'eighty percent' — present out of habit or obligation rather than genuine value, are: [list them]. Please help me design a Personal 20% Plan that: (1) Identifies 2–3 specific changes I could make in the next 30 days to invest more time in my personal Zone of Genius; (2) Helps me design an honest, compassionate strategy for reducing my lowest-value personal time commitments; (3) Suggests a simple weekly rhythm that protects time for what matters most."*

Endnotes: Oliver, M. (1992). New and Selected Poems. Boston: Beacon Press, chapter closing quote, p. 94. Thoreau, H.D. (1854). Walden, or Life in the Woods. Boston: Ticknor and Fields. Schwartz, B. (2004). The Paradox of Choice. New York: Ecco Press. Frankl, V. (1946/1984). Man's Search for Meaning. New York: Pocket Books. Csikszentmihalyi, M. (1997). Finding Flow: The Psychology of Engagement with Everyday Life. New York: Basic Books.

PART V

Your 30-Day Sprint

Knowledge without implementation is merely philosophy. Everything in the preceding fifteen chapters has been building toward this: thirty days of deliberate action that will move you from understanding your twenty percent to living it. This is not a chapter to read. It is a calendar to follow. Each week has a specific focus, a set of exercises, and a daily AI check-in prompt. Work through it in sequence, one week at a time, and you will end the thirty days with a measurably higher Twenty Percent Ratio and the structural foundations for continued growth.

CHAPTER

16

Your 30-Day Sprint

PART V

Week 1: Discover — Days 1–7

> *"Know thyself."*
> — The Delphic maxim, inscribed at the Temple of Apollo at Delphi (c. 6th century BCE), cited in Plato, Protagoras, 343b

The Foundation of All Progress

The first week of the thirty-day launch is devoted entirely to honest self-knowledge. Not self-improvement, self-knowledge. The temptation, for action-oriented professionals, is to skip the diagnostic phase and proceed directly to implementation. This impulse, while understandable, is counterproductive. The Amplification Framework cannot be effectively applied without a clear, honest, specific understanding of your current Zone of Genius, your current Twenty Percent Ratio, and the primary forces currently displacing your twenty-percent time.

Week One contains three sequential exercises, each building on the previous. Do not rush them. Do not attempt to do them all in a single session. Allow the insights from each to settle before proceeding to the next. The quality of everything that follows depends on the honesty and precision with which you complete this week.

Day 1–2: The Energy Audit

Begin the Energy Audit on Day One. As described in Chapter One, track every task you engage in for more than fifteen minutes across both working days, rating each Green (energizing), Yellow (neutral), or Red (draining). Complete the audit without analysis during these two days, simply track and rate, as honestly as you can.

On the evening of Day Two, review your log. Calculate the percentages. Write three sentences: what surprised you most, what confirmed something you already suspected, and what you are most unwilling to acknowledge. The third sentence is the most important.

Day 3–4: The 20% Fingerprint

Days Three and Four are devoted to the Zone of Genius diagnostic from Chapter Two. Work through the five diagnostic questions with genuine care. Share your answers with a trusted colleague or mentor and ask them to challenge any conclusions that seem self-flattering or incomplete. Construct your Twenty Percent Profile: a single, specific, honest statement of the activities, problems, and contexts in which you operate at your highest level.

The Twenty Percent Profile is not a wish list. It is not a description of the work you would like to be doing. It is a description of the work in which you are, right now, with the capabilities you currently possess, most extraordinary. This distinction matters enormously for the practical work ahead.

Day 5–7: The Calendar Autopsy

Using the Task Taxonomy from Chapter Four, apply the Calendar Autopsy to your actual calendar and task records from the past thirty days. Categorize every significant time expenditure into Category One through Four. Calculate your baseline Twenty Percent Ratio.

Record this number. It is your starting point. For most professionals completing this exercise for the first time, it will be between eight and fifteen percent. Whatever it is, it is not a verdict on your worth or your potential; it is a single data point, the first coordinate required before a course can be plotted.

You have named it. Now it is time to protect it. Weeks Two and Three are where intention becomes structure.

WEEK 1 DAILY CHECK-IN PROMPT

Use this prompt at the end of each day during Week 1 to track your ratio and identify one thing to shift tomorrow.

> *"End of day check-in. Today I worked on the following tasks for the following approximate amounts of time: [list tasks and time]. Please: (1) Categorize each task as 20% Genius Work, Necessary Infrastructure, Delegable, or Automatable; (2) Calculate today's approximate Twenty Percent Ratio; (3) Identify the single biggest 80% time drain from today; (4) Suggest one specific action I could take tomorrow to shift today's ratio upward by even 5%."*

Endnotes: Plato. Protagoras. (4th century BCE). Trans. C.C.W. Taylor. Oxford: Clarendon Press, 1976. Delphi inscription: Pausanias, Description of Greece, 10.24.1.

Weeks 2–3: Protect and Offload — Days 8–21

> *"Give me six hours to chop down a tree and I will spend the first four sharpening the axe."*
> — A preparedness maxim of uncertain origin, commonly circulated in management literature since the 1950s; no verified Lincoln source exists

From Diagnosis to Architecture

Armed with a clear Twenty Percent Profile and a baseline Twenty Percent Ratio, you are now ready to begin the structural work of the Amplification Framework: building the calendar architecture that protects your genius time and deliberately offloading the tasks that do not belong on your personal task list.

Weeks Two and Three are the most intensive of the thirty-day program. They require genuine decisions, about what you will stop doing, about what you will delegate, about how you will restructure your days, and about which AI-assisted workflows you will build and deploy. These decisions are not merely intellectual; they involve organizational relationships, established habits, and professional identities. Approach them with both determination and patience.

Week 2: The Fortress Calendar

Begin Week Two by redesigning your calendar. The Fortress Calendar design process proceeds in three steps. The first step is identification: mark, on your calendar template for the coming week, the blocks of time you will commit to Category One work, Zone of Genius activities that will be treated as inviolable appointments. For most professionals beginning this work, two or three blocks of ninety minutes per week is a realistic starting point for deep work protection.

The second step is the Meeting Audit: review every recurring meeting on your calendar and apply three questions. First, does this meeting require my Zone of Genius to be present, or merely my authority or organizational role? Second, could the outcome of this meeting be achieved through asynchronous communication? Third, if this meeting is genuinely necessary, could it be shorter, less frequent, or attended only for the portion that requires my input? Act on the answers to these questions with concrete changes to your calendar.

The third step is the Fortress Defense Protocol: establish, and communicate to your immediate colleagues, the ground rules for your protected deep work blocks. This need not be dramatic; a simple statement — 'I keep Tuesday and Thursday mornings clear for focused work on our major priorities and am available by message or in the afternoon for everything else' — is sufficient in most organizational cultures.

Week 3: The 10-Day Offload Challenge

The ten working days of Weeks Two and Three constitute the Offload Sprint: a structured challenge in which you identify and initiate the transfer of at least one recurring task per day from your personal task list to a delegate, an AI system, or an automated process. Over ten days, you will have begun the transfer of at least ten tasks, which, based on typical time expenditures per task, should recover between five and fifteen hours of weekly working time.

The key word is 'begun.' The Offload Sprint is not about instantly and perfectly delegating ten tasks; it is about initiating ten delegation processes, each of which will require some ongoing refinement. The goal of Week Three is to get the transfers in motion: to brief the delegates, to write the AI prompts, to design the automated processes, and to accept that the first iteration of each delegation will be imperfect.

> *"Done is better than perfect."*
>
> — Sheryl Sandberg, Lean In (2013), p. 125

First AI Offloads

For professionals new to systematic AI use, Week Three is the ideal moment to deploy their first three AI offload workflows. Based on the task categorization from Week One, select the three Category Four (Automatable) tasks that currently consume the most time, and design specific AI prompts or workflows to handle each one. Run each workflow three times in the first week, reviewing outputs and refining prompts after each iteration.

The three AI offload workflows most commonly identified as highest-value in this sprint are: email triage and draft responses, meeting agenda preparation and post-meeting summarization, and first-draft production for recurring report or communication formats. Each of these, once properly designed, can be reliably automated within a week and can recover between two and five hours per week.

The fortress is built. The eighty percent is moving. Week Four is where you measure what has changed and decide what you are building next.

WEEKLY STRATEGY PROMPT, Weeks 2–3

Use this prompt at the end of each week to review what displaced your genius time and redesign the following week's calendar.

> *"Weekly strategy review. Here is how last week's calendar actually unfolded versus my plan: [describe]. Here were my top wins: [list]. Here were my biggest 80% traps, the things that displaced my planned genius-work time: [list]. Here is my current Twenty Percent Ratio estimate: [X%]. Please: (1) Analyze what prevented me from achieving my planned protected deep work time; (2) Identify the top two specific structural changes I should make to next week's calendar to better protect my genius blocks; (3) Suggest the next delegation or automation I should implement this week; (4) Design next week's ideal Fortress Calendar, treating my three genius blocks as sacred."*

Endnotes: Lincoln quotation: extensive research by Quote Investigator (quoteinvestigator.com) finds no reliable attribution. Sandberg, S. (2013). Lean In: Women, Work, and the Will to Lead. New York: Alfred A. Knopf, p. 125. Covey, S. (1989). The 7 Habits of Highly Effective People. New York: Free Press.

Week 4: Amplify and Sustain — Days 22–30

The Transition from Sprint to System

The fourth week of the launch marks a transition in the nature of the work. Weeks One through Three were characterized by intensity: intensive diagnosis, intensive structural redesign, intensive delegation and automation. Week Four is characterized by consolidation: reflecting on what has changed, celebrating what has worked, examining what has not, and, most importantly, designing the systems that will sustain and extend the gains beyond the thirty-day sprint.

The central risk at Week Four is backslide. Research on behavioral change shows that new habits are most vulnerable not at the start, when motivation is high, but in the weeks after the initial sprint — when momentum has faded but the behavior has not yet become automatic. This is the backslide window. The professional who has successfully protected three deep work blocks per week during the sprint faces a different risk in Week Four than in Week One: not resistance but complacency. The systems designed in Week Four are the antidote.

Measuring Your Progress

Before designing Week Four's sustainability systems, take stock with precision. Calculate your current Twenty Percent Ratio from the past two weeks' time logs. Compare it to your baseline from Week One. Document the specific changes that contributed most to the improvement. Identify the three areas where you made the least progress and analyze why.

For most professionals completing the thirty-day launch, the Week Four Twenty Percent Ratio is between eighteen and thirty percent, an improvement of approximately one to two times the baseline. This is meaningful progress. It is also a long way from the forty-plus percent that represents the genuine amplification of genius that this framework is designed to achieve. Week Four is not the end of the journey; it is the end of the beginning.

The 90-Day Genius Plan

The primary deliverable of Week Four is the 90-Day Genius Plan — a structured, calendar-backed commitment to the next phase of Twenty Percent Ratio improvement. Not a vision statement. Not a list of intentions.

It answers four questions: What is my current ratio? What is my ninety-day target? What three to five specific changes will I make to get there? And who will I share this plan with to create accountability?

The Accountability System

James Clear, in Atomic Habits, draws on behavioral science to show that the sustainability of behavioral change depends critically on environmental design, on structuring the environment so that the desired behaviors are easier to perform than the undesired ones, and so that the social context supports rather than undermines the change. For the twenty-percent professional, the most important element of the accountability system is a regular, structured review of Twenty

Percent Ratio performance, ideally weekly, and ideally with an accountability partner who understands the framework.

The Weekly Twenty Percent Review need take no more than fifteen minutes: reviewing the weeks' time log, calculating the ratio, identifying the primary determinants of that week's performance, and setting a specific intention for the following week. Done consistently, this fifteen-minute review is the most powerful single practice available for sustaining long term progress in Twenty Percent Ratio.

> *"You do not rise to the level of your goals. You fall to the level of your systems."*
> — James Clear, Atomic Habits (2018), p. 27

A Closing Reflection

The twenty-percent principle, at its deepest level, is not a productivity framework. It is a statement about the purpose of work and, more broadly, about the purpose of a professional life. The premise underlying every technique, every exercise, and every AI prompt in this book is a simple but profound one: that you are here, in this role, in this field, with the particular constellation of talents and experiences you have accumulated, for a reason, and that the reason is connected to your Zone of Genius.

The work you do in your Zone of Genius is not merely more productive than the work you do in your Zone of Excellence or your Zone of Competence. It is more real. It is more distinctively yours. It is the work that, when you look back on your career from a significant distance, you will recognize as the work that mattered. The work that changed something, solved something, helped someone in a way only you could have.

The eighty percent is not the enemy. It is simply the cost of organizational life, to be managed with intelligence and reduced with discipline. The twenty percent is the point. Protect it, deepen it, and let it be what carries you forward.

Somewhere in China, in a park, there is still a sign. Tiny grass, still dreaming.

The person who made it had a tool. A powerful one. What they did not have was knowledge of the destination — a clear enough picture of the result to know when the output had gone wrong.

You now have both. Thirty days ago you picked up this book with a ratio and a vague sense that something important was being crowded out of your working life. You leave it with a map, a system, a set of tools, and — most importantly — a precise understanding of the work that only you can do.

That understanding is the destination. AI can carry you toward it faster than anything else available to a professional today. But it cannot know the destination for you. It cannot tell you which grass is yours, or what it means for it to dream.

That part has always been yours. It still is.

Your twenty percent does not stop here — you amplify it.

30-DAY REVIEW PROMPT, Week 4

Use this prompt at the end of your thirty-day sprint to measure how far you have come and design the next ninety days.

> *"I have just completed my 30-Day 20% Launch. Here is my summary: My baseline Twenty Percent Ratio was [X%]. My current ratio is [Y%]. The three changes that made the biggest difference were: [list them]. The biggest obstacles I encountered were: [list them]. The one insight that surprised me most was: [describe it]. Based on this, please help me design my 90-Day Genius Plan by: (1) Recommending a realistic but ambitious Target Ratio for 90 days from now; (2) Suggesting the three most important structural commitments to sustain and extend my progress; (3) Identifying the single highest-leverage next offload or automation I should prioritize; (4) Designing a simple weekly review protocol I will actually use; (5) Writing a brief statement of intention I can return to whenever my twenty-percent practice needs renewal."*

Endnotes: Clear, J. (2018). Atomic Habits: An Easy & Proven Way to Build Good Habits & Break Bad Ones. New York: Avery. Duhigg, C. (2012). The Power of Habit. New York: Random House. Prochaska, J. & DiClemente, C. (1984). The Transtheoretical Approach. Homewood, IL: Dow Jones-Irwin.

Bibliography

The following works are cited in the text or have materially influenced the thinking in this book. Where multiple editions exist, the edition cited in the text is specified.

Primary Works Cited

[] Amabile, T. & Kramer, S. (2011). The Progress Principle: Using Small Wins to Ignite Joy, Engagement, and Creativity at Work. Boston: Harvard Business Review Press.

[] Einstein, A. & Infeld, L. (1938). The Evolution of Physics: The Growth of Ideas from Early Concepts to Relativity and Quanta. New York: Simon & Schuster. [Chapter 4 and Chapter 11 epigraphs, verified source, p. 92.]

[] James, W. (1890). The Principles of Psychology, 2 vols. New York: Henry Holt. [Chapter 5 epigraph, verified source, Vol. 1, p. 424.]

[] Oliver, M. (1992). New and Selected Poems. Boston: Beacon Press. [Chapter 15 closing quote — 'The Summer Day,' p. 94.]

[] Clear, J. (2018). Atomic Habits: An Easy & Proven Way to Build Good Habits & Break Bad Ones. New York: Avery/Penguin Random House.

[] Csikszentmihalyi, M. (1990). Flow: The Psychology of Optimal Experience. New York: Harper & Row. (10th anniversary edition, 2008, Harper Perennial.)

|| Csikszentmihalyi, M. (1997). Finding Flow: The Psychology of Engagement with Everyday Life. New York: Basic Books.

|| Deci, E. & Ryan, R. (2000). The 'What' and 'Why' of Goal Pursuits: Human Needs and the Self-Determination of Behavior. Psychological Inquiry, 11(4), 227–268.

|| Dewey, J. (1910). How We Think. Boston: D.C. Heath & Co.

|| Drucker, P.F. (1966). The Effective Executive. New York: Harper & Row. (Revised edition, 2002, HarperBusiness.)

|| Duhigg, C. (2012). The Power of Habit: Why We Do What We Do in Life and Business. New York: Random House.

|| Edmondson, A.C. (1999). Psychological Safety and Learning Behavior in Work Teams. Administrative Science Quarterly, 44(2), 350–383.

|| Edmondson, A.C. (2018). The Fearless Organization: Creating Psychological Safety in the Workplace for Learning, Innovation, and Growth. Hoboken: Wiley.

|| Ericsson, A. & Pool, R. (2016). Peak: Secrets from the New Science of Expertise. Boston: Eamon Dolan/Houghton Mifflin Harcourt.

|| Fogg, B.J. (2019). Tiny Habits: The Small Changes That Change Everything. Boston: Houghton Mifflin Harcourt.

|| Frankl, V.E. (1946). Man's Search for Meaning. (English translation, 1959. Boston: Beacon Press. Pocket Books edition, 1984.)

|| Gates, B. (1999). Business @ the Speed of Thought: Using a Digital Nervous System. New York: Warner Books.

|| Gollwitzer, P. (1999). Implementation Intentions: Strong Effects of Simple Plans. American Psychologist, 54(7), 493–503.

|| Grant, A. (2013). Give and Take: A Revolutionary Approach to Success. New York: Viking/Penguin.

|| Hendricks, G. (2009). The Big Leap: Conquer Your Hidden Fear and Take Life to the Next Level. New York: HarperOne.

|| Huffington, A. (2016). The Sleep Revolution: Transforming Your Life, One Night at a Time. New York: Harmony Books.

|| Ibarra, H. (2003). Working Identity: Unconventional Strategies for Reinventing Your Career. Boston: Harvard Business School Press.

|| Jackson, T., Dawson, R. & Wilson, D. (2003). Reducing the Effect of Email Interruptions on Employees. International Journal of Information Management, 23(1), 55–65.

|| Kahneman, D. (2011). Thinking, Fast and Slow. New York: Farrar, Straus and Giroux.

|| Keller, G. & Papasan, J. (2012). The One Thing: The Surprisingly Simple Truth Behind Extraordinary Results. Austin: Bard Press.

|| Kelly, K. (2016). The Inevitable: Understanding the 12 Technological Forces That Will Shape Our Future. New York: Viking.

|| Koch, R. (1997). The 80/20 Principle: The Secret to Achieving More with Less. London: Nicholas Brealey. (Revised edition, 2008.)

|| Lencioni, P. (2002). The Five Dysfunctions of a Team. San Francisco: Jossey-Bass.

|| Levitin, D. (2014). The Organized Mind: Thinking Straight in the Age of Information Overload. New York: Dutton.

[] Loehr, J. & Schwartz, T. (2003). The Power of Full Engagement: Managing Energy, Not Time, Is the Key to High Performance and Personal Renewal. New York: Free Press.

[] Mark, G., Gonzalez, V. & Harris, J. (2005). No Task Left Behind? Examining the Nature of Fragmented Work. Proceedings of the SIGCHI Conference on Human Factors in Computing Systems (CHI 2005), 321–330.

[] Newport, C. (2016). Deep Work: Rules for Focused Success in a Distracted World. New York: Grand Central Publishing.

[] Nonaka, I. & Takeuchi, H. (1995). The Knowledge-Creating Company: How Japanese Companies Create the Dynamics of Innovation. New York: Oxford University Press.

[] Peter, L.J. & Hull, R. (1969). The Peter Principle: Why Things Always Go Wrong. New York: William Morrow.

[] Pink, D. (2009). Drive: The Surprising Truth About What Motivates Us. New York: Riverhead Books.

[] Polanyi, M. (1966). The Tacit Dimension. New York: Doubleday.

[] Rogelberg, S. (2019). The Surprising Science of Meetings: How You Can Lead Your Team to Peak Performance. New York: Oxford University Press.

[] Russell, S. & Norvig, P. (2021). Artificial Intelligence: A Modern Approach (4th ed.). Hoboken: Pearson.

[] Schwartz, B. (2004). The Paradox of Choice: Why More Is Less. New York: Ecco Press.

[] Senge, P. (1990). The Fifth Discipline: The Art and Practice of the Learning Organization. New York: Currency/Doubleday.

[] Thoreau, H.D. (1854). Walden, or Life in the Woods. Boston: Ticknor and Fields.

[] Aristotle. Metaphysics. Trans. W.D. Ross. Book H, 1045a.8–10. Oxford: Clarendon Press, 1924. [Chapter 8 epigraph.]

[] Sandberg, S. (2013). Lean In: Women, Work, and the Will to Lead. New York: Alfred A. Knopf. [Chapter 16 sprint section epigraph, p. 125.]

[] White, J. et al. (2023). A Prompt Pattern Catalog to Enhance Prompt Engineering with ChatGPT. arXiv:2302.11382.

Further Reading

[] Baumeister, R. & Tierney, J. (2011). Willpower: Rediscovering the Greatest Human Strength. New York: Penguin Press.

[] Brynjolfsson, E. & McAfee, A. (2014). The Second Machine Age: Work, Progress, and Prosperity in a Time of Brilliant Technologies. New York: W.W. Norton.

[] Buckingham, M. & Clifton, D. (2001). Now, Discover Your Strengths. New York: Free Press.

[] Covey, S.R. (1989). The 7 Habits of Highly Effective People. New York: Free Press.

[] Covey, S.R. (1994). First Things First. New York: Simon & Schuster.

[] Grant, A. (2021). Think Again: The Power of Knowing What You Don't Know. New York: Viking.

[] Kissinger, H. (2022). Leadership: Six Studies in World Strategy. New York: Penguin Press.

[] Taleb, N.N. (2012). Antifragile: Things That Gain from Disorder. New York: Random House.

APPENDIX

The Complete AI Prompt Library

The following is a complete, consolidated reference of every AI prompt and agent specification included in this book, organized by chapter. Each prompt is designed to be used with any capable large language model, Claude, ChatGPT, Gemini, or their successors. Where you see text in [brackets], replace the bracketed placeholder with your own specific information before submitting.

These prompts are most effective when treated as templates rather than scripts. Read the surrounding chapter before deploying each prompt so that you understand the conceptual purpose it serves. A prompt used without that context is a tool used without understanding its function. A prompt used with full context is a lever that can move remarkable weight.

For ongoing use, the author recommends building a personal prompt library, a living document or notes application in which you store, refine, and expand these prompts as you develop your own working relationship with AI tools. Chapter Eleven describes the method for doing this in detail.

PART ONE:

The 80/20 Truth Nobody Tells You

Chapter 1, The Exhaustion Equation

Purpose: Identify which of today's tasks are energy-generating versus energy-draining, and surface quick wins for delegation or automation.

DAILY ENERGY TRIAGE PROMPT

> *"Review my task list for today: [paste your complete task list]. For each item, assess whether this type of task is typically energy-generating, energy-neutral, or energy-draining for a professional whose primary strengths are [describe 2–3 of your core strengths in specific terms]. For any energy-draining task, suggest whether it could be (a) delegated to a colleague or direct report, (b) handled by an AI assistant using a well-designed prompt, (c) eliminated entirely without meaningful consequence, or (d) batched with similar tasks to reduce context-switching cost. Be specific and direct in your recommendations."*

Chapter 2, What Is Your 20%?

Purpose: Identify the patterns that constitute your Zone of Genius by analyzing your proudest professional moments.

ZONE OF GENIUS DISCOVERY PROMPT

> *"I am going to describe three recent professional moments I am genuinely proud of: [describe each one in 3–5 sentences, including what you were doing, what made it feel different, and what the outcome was]. After reviewing all three, please: (1) Identify the common themes, capabilities, and types of problems that appear across all three examples; (2) Articulate what appears to be my Zone of Genius, the specific type of work in which my unique combination of skill and energy seems to be at its highest; (3) Ask me five targeted follow-up questions that will help me sharpen and validate this picture with greater precision."*

Chapter 3, The Tyranny of the 80%

Purpose: Audit your recent calendar to quantify how much time is genuinely spent in Zone of Genius work versus displacement activities.

CALENDAR AUTOPSY PROMPT

> *"Here is my calendar and task log from the past two weeks: [paste your schedule in text form, or describe the recurring categories of meetings and tasks by day]. Please analyze this schedule by categorizing each recurring activity type as: (A) 20% Genius Work, requires my unique capabilities and judgment; (B) Necessary Infrastructure, must be done but does not require my unique genius; (C) Delegable, required my authority or title but not my unique skills; (D) Automatable, rule-governed, repetitive, and suitable for AI or process handling. After categorizing, calculate my approximate Twenty Percent Ratio for these two weeks, then identify the top three highest-value changes I could make immediately to recover time for Category A work."*

PART TWO:

The Amplification Framework

Chapter 4, Stage 1: MAP

Purpose: Categorize every recurring responsibility in your role and calculate your baseline Twenty Percent Ratio.

TASK TAXONOMY MAPPING PROMPT

> *"Act as my productivity strategist. I am going to share all of the recurring tasks and responsibilities that make up my role: [list them in as much detail as possible, include frequency, approximate time per occurrence, and what the output or purpose of each task is]. Your task: categorize each one as (A) Core Genius Work requiring my unique capabilities, (B) Necessary Infrastructure that must be done but does not require my unique genius, (C) Delegable Responsibilities that need my authority but not my unique skills, or (D) Automatable Processes that are rule-governed and repetitive. After categorizing all items: (1) Calculate my current approximate Twenty Percent Ratio; (2) Identify the top three Category C or D tasks I should address first to recover the most time; (3) Suggest one practical, specific first step to begin the transition for each of those three tasks."*

Chapter 5, Stage 2: PROTECT

Purpose: An ongoing weekly agent that reviews your schedule and defends your genius-work time against displacement.

CALENDAR GUARDIAN AGENT PROMPT

> *"You are my calendar guardian. I will share my planned schedule with you each Monday morning. Your ongoing mission is to: (1) Identify all blocks of genuine 20% Genius Work already protected in the schedule and confirm they are adequately defended; (2) Flag any meeting that could plausibly be handled asynchronously, provide a draft message I could send to replace it; (3) Identify any full working day with no protected deep work time, and suggest where a 90-minute block could be carved out; (4) Propose a revised weekly schedule that protects at least three uninterrupted 90-minute blocks for my core genius work. My Zone of Genius is: [describe your 20% in specific terms]. My peak cognitive hours are typically: [specify your best hours, e.g., 8–11am]. This week's schedule is: [paste your calendar]."*

Chapter 6, Stage 3: OFFLOAD

Purpose: Design a complete handoff system, including SOP, AI automation, and quality audit, for any recurring task you want to remove from your personal plate.

DELEGATION AND AUTOMATION DESIGN PROMPT

> *"I have a recurring task I currently handle personally that I want to systematically offload. The task is: [describe it in full detail, include what triggers it, what inputs are required, what decisions are made, what the output looks like, and approximately how long it takes each time]. Please help me design a complete offload system by: (1) Writing a detailed Standard Operating Procedure (SOP) I could give to a team member or virtual assistant, include every step, decision point, and quality standard; (2) Identifying any component of this task that could be handled entirely by AI, with no meaningful quality loss; (3) Writing the exact AI prompt(s) I would use for those AI-handled components, make them ready to use immediately; (4) Designing a simple quality audit process I could use to verify the work is being done to my standard once it is off my plate. Be thorough and specific."*

Chapter 7, Stage 4: AMPLIFY

Purpose: Design a 90-day deliberate practice roadmap for going deeper into your Zone of Genius.

GENIUS DEPTH DEVELOPMENT PROMPT

"My Zone of Genius, as I currently understand it, is: [describe in specific, concrete terms, include the types of problems, the capabilities deployed, and the contexts in which you do your best work]. I want to go significantly deeper in this area over the next 90 days, not broader, but deeper. Please design a specific Deliberate Practice Roadmap for me that includes: (1) The three most important sub-capabilities within my genius zone that I should develop to move from very good to genuinely extraordinary; (2) Specific practice activities I can integrate into my actual work, not separate from it, to develop each sub-capability; (3) A simple weekly measurement system for tracking whether each capability is improving; (4) Suggested reading, study, or professional exposure that would most accelerate development in this area; (5) One person in my professional network who likely has deep expertise in this domain, and a suggested approach for pursuing a structured mentoring relationship with them."

Chapter 8, Stage 5: SCALE

Purpose: Design a knowledge transfer system that extends your Zone of Genius beyond your individual output to your team.

GENIUS SCALING AND KNOWLEDGE TRANSFER PROMPT

> *"I want to systematically scale my expertise in [describe your Zone of Genius specifically] so that my team can access and apply it without being entirely dependent on my direct involvement in every situation. Help me design a Knowledge Transfer System by specifying: (1) The three most important dimensions of my expertise that I should document first, including what format would make each dimension most practically useful for my team; (2) A teaching format I could use regularly to share this knowledge with my team, for example, weekly case reviews, annotated examples of my decision-making process, or structured coaching conversations; (3) How AI tools could help my team access my expertise asynchronously, for example, through a custom AI assistant configured with my principles, frameworks, and decision heuristics; (4) Specific metrics I could track over 90 days to evaluate whether the knowledge transfer is actually working and reducing dependence on me personally."*

PART THREE:

AI as Your 20% Multiplier

Chapter 9, Rethinking AI: Your 80% Slayer

Purpose: Establish your AI Chief of Staff, a standing relationship prompt that orients every AI interaction around protecting and amplifying your 20%.

AI CHIEF OF STAFF SETUP PROMPT

> *"You are my personal AI Chief of Staff. Your ongoing mission is to help me spend as much of my working time as possible in my Zone of Genius, which I define as: [describe your 20% in specific, concrete terms, include the types of problems, the capabilities you deploy, and what distinguishes your highest-value contributions]. Every time I bring you a task, your first diagnostic question should be: 'Does this task actually require your unique expertise, judgment, and perspective?' If the honest answer is no, your job is to either handle it yourself, help me design a delegation to a colleague, or create a system so it is handled automatically in the future without requiring my attention. Begin our relationship by asking me five questions that will help you understand my role, my organizational context, my key relationships, and my working preferences deeply enough to serve this mission effectively."*

Chapter 10, Building Your AI Workflow Stack (part 1)

Purpose: Start every working day with clarity, delegation, and a protected plan for your most important work.

MORNING RITUAL PROMPT

> *"Good morning. I want to begin this day with clarity and intention. Here are the three most important outcomes I need to achieve today: [list them in order of priority]. Here is everything else currently on my task list and in my inbox: [list all tasks and pending items, or paste your inbox summary]. Please: (1) Confirm which items on my full task list align directly with my top three outcomes, and which do not; (2) For any item you can handle or draft on my behalf with no further input from me, write a first draft or complete response right now; (3) Identify any items that should be delegated and to whom, write a brief delegation message for each; (4) Flag anything that requires my direct personal attention before my first deep work session, which begins at [time]; (5) Design a time-blocked schedule for today that protects at least [number] hours for my top three priorities and addresses everything else efficiently."*

Chapter 10, Building Your AI Workflow Stack (part 2)

Purpose: Review the past week, analyze performance, and redesign the following week for maximum Twenty Percent Ratio.

WEEKLY AI REVIEW PROMPT

> *"Weekly strategy review. Here is how last week's calendar actually unfolded, compared to what I planned: [describe what happened, what got done, what got displaced, what surprised you]. Here were my top three wins from last week: [list them]. Here were the top three 80% traps, the things that most displaced my planned genius-work time: [list them with specific context]. My estimated Twenty Percent Ratio for last week was approximately: [X%]. Based on this review, please: (1) Analyze the primary structural or behavioral factors that prevented me from achieving my planned protected deep work time; (2) Identify the top two specific, practical changes to make to next week's calendar or workflow to better protect my genius blocks; (3) Suggest the next delegation or automation I should implement this week to recover additional 80% time; (4) Design next week's ideal Fortress Calendar, treating my genius work blocks as non-negotiable appointments."*

Chapter 11, Prompt Design for 20% Thinkers

Purpose: Build a complete Personal Prompt Library tailored to your specific role and highest-value tasks.

PERSONAL PROMPT LIBRARY BUILDER

"I want to build a Personal Prompt Library for my role as [your title and a brief description of your function]. My five most frequent high-value tasks, the ones where I most need AI assistance that is actually calibrated to my working style, are: [list all five in specific terms, including what the typical input looks like and what a great output looks like]. For each of the five tasks, please write a reusable, high-quality prompt template using the SCOPE framework (Situation, Context, Output, Parameters, Examples). Each template must: (1) Establish the appropriate AI role and framing for that type of task; (2) Include clearly marked placeholders in [square brackets] for the variable information I will fill in each time I use it; (3) Specify the exact output format, length, and tone that would be most immediately useful to me; (4) Include any standing constraints, standards, or preferences that apply to this category of work; (5) Reflect how I actually think and communicate, not generic professional language. Write a complete, ready-to-use template for each of the five tasks."

Chapter 12, AI Agents: Your Always-On 80% Team

Purpose: Design a complete specification for an AI agent to handle a specific recurring task autonomously.

AI AGENT DESIGN PROMPT

"I want to design an AI agent that handles [describe the specific recurring task in full detail, what it is, what triggers it, what inputs are required, and what the output should look like] for me automatically and reliably. This task currently takes me approximately [X hours] per week. Please help me design this agent by specifying: (1) Exactly what information inputs the agent needs each time it runs to complete the task to a high standard; (2) A complete step-by-step workflow the agent should follow, including every decision point, sub-task, and output it should produce along the way; (3) A clear specification of which decisions the agent should make autonomously versus which it should escalate to me for review, including the specific criteria for escalation; (4) A sample output template showing exactly what the agent's completed work product should look like; (5) How I would measure and evaluate the agent's performance quality on an ongoing basis; (6) What tools, data sources, or system integrations the agent would need to function effectively."

PART FOUR:

The 20% Life

Chapter 13, The 20% Leader

Purpose: Design a team-level 20% strategy, including discovery conversations, a Genius Map, and a reallocation plan.

TEAM GENIUS MAP DESIGN PROMPT

> *"I manage a team of [number] people. Their roles are: [briefly describe each person's role and primary responsibilities]. I want to help each person spend more time in their individual Zone of Genius and less time on work that does not require their highest capabilities. Please help me design a complete Team 20% Strategy by creating: (1) A complete 1:1 conversation framework, specific questions I can use with each team member to discover their Zone of Genius, identify where their current role aligns with it, and surface where they feel most and least energized; (2) A simple visual format for capturing each person's profile and sharing the Team Genius Map with the group; (3) A practical 90-day plan for progressively restructuring task allocation across the team, including how to handle the tasks being vacated and how to manage the transition without disrupting performance; (4) Two or three specific metrics I could track to measure whether the team's collective Twenty Percent Ratio is improving over the next quarter."*

Chapter 14, The 20% Career

Purpose: Analyze your career trajectory through the 20% lens and design a path toward a role with a higher genius ratio.

CAREER AMPLIFICATION DESIGN PROMPT

> *"I want to design a career trajectory that moves me progressively toward spending at least 50% of my working time in my Zone of Genius within the next three years. My Zone of Genius is: [describe it specifically, the types of problems, the capabilities, and the work that makes you feel most alive and most effective]. My current role is: [describe your title, responsibilities, and organizational context]. My estimated current Twenty Percent Ratio is approximately: [X%]. The biggest structural barriers preventing me from a higher ratio are: [list 2–3 specific things, meetings, responsibilities, organizational expectations, etc.]. Please help me: (1) Analyze precisely where the gap is between my current role and my twenty-percent ideal; (2) Identify three to five possible career moves, including lateral moves, role evolution within my current organization, and conventional promotion paths, that would increase my genius ratio rather than decrease it; (3) Develop a credible business case I could present to my current leadership for restructuring my role to better align with my highest-value contributions; (4) Identify specific steps I could take in the next 90 days to make my Zone of Genius more visible and legible to the organizational decision-makers who shape my career."*

Chapter 15, The 20% Life

Purpose: Apply the 80/20 lens to the full canvas of your life, not just your professional role, and design a personal plan for protecting what matters most.

FULL LIFE AMPLIFICATION PROMPT

> *"I want to apply the 80/20 principle to my whole life, not just my professional work. My three to five core personal values, the things I believe life is actually for, are: [list them honestly]. The activities, relationships, and pursuits in my personal life that genuinely call upon my deepest capacities and create the most meaning are: [list them with brief explanations of why each matters]. The obligations, habits, and time commitments in my personal life that feel like my personal 'eighty percent' — things that are present out of habit, social obligation, or inertia rather than genuine alignment with my values, are: [list them honestly]. Please help me design a Personal 20% Life Plan that: (1) Identifies two to three specific changes I could make in the next 30 days to invest more time in the personal activities and relationships that most deeply call upon who I am at my best; (2) Proposes an honest, compassionate strategy for reducing my lowest-value personal time commitments, without damaging important relationships or abandoning genuine responsibilities; (3) Designs a simple sustainable weekly rhythm that reliably protects time for what matters most."*

PART FIVE:

Your 30-Day Sprint

Chapter 16, Your 30-Day Sprint

Purpose: A daily check-in during discovery week to track your energy ratio and identify one improvement each day.

WEEK 1 DAILY CHECK-IN PROMPT

> *"End-of-day check-in for my 20% Launch. Today I worked on the following tasks for approximately these amounts of time: [list each task and your best time estimate]. Please: (1) Categorize each task as 20% Genius Work, Necessary Infrastructure, Delegable, or Automatable; (2) Calculate today's approximate Twenty Percent Ratio as a percentage; (3) Identify the single biggest 80% time drain from today, the item that displaced the most genius-work potential; (4) Suggest one specific, practical step I could take tomorrow to shift today's ratio upward by even five percentage points. Keep your response concise and direct, I am building a daily habit, not a weekly report."*

Chapter 16, Weeks 2–3: Protect and Offload

Purpose: A structured weekly strategy session to review last week's performance, identify what went wrong, and design next week's Fortress Calendar.

WEEKLY FORTRESS CALENDAR PROMPT

"Weekly strategy review for my 20% Launch. Here is how last week's schedule actually unfolded: [describe what happened, be honest about what displaced your planned deep work blocks]. Here were my top wins from last week: [list them]. Here were the top 80% traps that displaced my planned genius time: [list them with specific context about why they happened]. My estimated Twenty Percent Ratio for last week was approximately: [X%]. Please: (1) Analyze the primary reason my planned protected deep work time was not fully defended; (2) Identify the top two structural changes I should make to next week's calendar to better protect my genius blocks; (3) Name the single next delegation or automation I should implement this week, and write the delegation message or AI prompt for it; (4) Design next week's Fortress Calendar with my three genius work blocks marked as immovable, and everything else organized around them."

Chapter 16, Week 4: Amplify and Sustain

Purpose: A comprehensive 30-day review that captures what changed, what you learned, and designs the next 90-day phase of your amplification practice.

30-DAY REVIEW AND 90-DAY GENIUS PLAN PROMPT

"I have just completed my 30-Day 20% Launch. Here is my full review: My baseline Twenty Percent Ratio at the start was approximately [X%]. My current ratio after 30 days is approximately [Y%]. The three changes that made the biggest measurable difference were: [list them with brief explanations]. The biggest obstacles I encountered, the things that most resisted change, were: [list them honestly]. The one insight that surprised me most during this process was: [describe it]. Based on this review, please help me design my 90-Day Genius Plan by: (1) Recommending a specific, realistic but ambitious target Twenty Percent Ratio for 90 days from now, with a brief rationale; (2) Specifying the three most important structural commitments I must sustain and extend to reach that target, with enough specificity that I can put them on a calendar; (3) Identifying the single highest-leverage next offload or automation I should prioritize in the first two weeks of the new phase; (4) Designing a simple weekly review protocol, no more than 15 minutes, that I will realistically maintain; (5) Writing a brief personal statement of intention, two to three sentences, that I can return to whenever my 20% practice needs renewal."

A Note on Prompt Refinement

No prompt in this library should be treated as final. Every prompt is a starting hypothesis about how to get useful output from an AI system for a particular type of task. As you use these prompts, you'll discover that some produce output requiring little refinement, others require significant editing, and a few may not work as intended for your specific context until you have adjusted the framing, the output specification, or the standing context.

The discipline of iterative prompt refinement, reviewing each prompt after use, noting where the output fell short of what you needed, and making one targeted adjustment before the next use, is itself a Zone of Genius practice: it requires precisely the kind of analytical attention and precise language that distinguishes expert from novice knowledge workers. As you build your Personal Prompt Library over time, you're not just accumulating tools. You are developing a new dimension of professional capability.

The prompts in this appendix are available in digital format for easy copying and customization. Visit Andrew Ram Bittan's professional profiles for updates, new prompt templates, and additional resources as the AI landscape continues to evolve.

linkedin.com/in/andrewbittan

About the Author

Andrew Ram Bittan is a Maryland native who holds an MBA from the prestigious Johns Hopkins University and is a business strategist who has spent more than thirty years asking the same question in every organization he has entered: where is the genius being wasted, and what would it take to set it free?

His career has taken him across enterprise technology, healthcare IT, government, and education — training practitioners, building partner ecosystems, redesigning clinical workflows, and advising institutions on how to deploy intelligence, human and artificial, where it creates the most impact. He is the creator of the BPIA Framework™, a consulting methodology integrating Business Intelligence, Process Intelligence, and Artificial Intelligence that has been tested against the kinds of organizational problems that resist easy solutions. It is the foundation of his advisory practice, Miraivant.

A teacher becomes a student and a student becomes a teacher — the cycle of learning never ends. I hope the ideas in these pages truly help you find your full potential. Your 20%, amplified.

Connect with Andrew

linkedin.com/in/andrewbittan · miraivant.com

Special Thanks

I would like to thank the following people for lending their expertise and guidance during the review process of this book.

David Holzel

Erica Simmons

Howard Mei

www.ingramcontent.com/pod-product-compliance
Lightning Source LLC
LaVergne TN
LVHW050535100826
845148LV00002B/570

9798234067630